BURGESS-CARPENTER LIBRARY
ROOM 406 BUTLER LIBRARY
COLUMBIA UNIVERSITY
NEW YORK 27, N. Y.

Hans Conzelmann

Jesus

The classic article from *RGG*[3]
expanded and updated

Translated by J. RAYMOND LORD

Edited, with an Introduction, by
JOHN REUMANN

WITHDRAWN

FORTRESS PRESS Philadelphia

Burgess
BT
202
.C6713

c. 1

This book is a translation of "Jesus Christus," published in *Die Religion in Geschichte und Gegenwart: Handwörterbuch für Theologie und Religionswissenschaft,* ed. Kurt Galling et al. (Tübingen: J. C. B. Mohr [Paul Siebeck]), vol. 3 (1959), cols. 619–53. It is translated here by arrangement with the University of Chicago Press, holder of the rights to English translation of *RGG,* and with J. C. B. Mohr (Paul Siebeck), Tübingen.

COPYRIGHT © 1973 BY FORTRESS PRESS

All rights reserved. No part of this publication may be reproduced, stored in a retrieval system, or transmitted in any form or by any means, electronic, mechanical, photocopying, recording, or otherwise, without the prior permission of the copyright owner.

Library of Congress Catalog Card Number 73-79011

ISBN 0-8006-1000-8

3310 C 73   Printed in U.S.A.   1-1000

NPB
SEP 20 1974

Contents

Editor's Introduction

"A MASTERFUL SUMMARY and presentation" is the way
Norman Perrin once described the article which follows on Jesus Christ, a translation appearing for the
first time in English from the definitive German Protestant encyclopedia, *Die Religion in Geschichte und
Gegenwart*. "Conzelmann set out to provide a review
of the current position in Life of Christ research, and
he succeeded admirably," Perrin went on. It is "a
presentation of the factors involved in this research
that should become a standard, a basis for future work
as the perspective from which he starts becomes even
more widely accepted" (*Rediscovering the Teaching
of Jesus* [New York: Harper & Row, 1967], pp. 250
and 42).

It is an article, Professor Perrin added, "which
demands both translation into English and presentation in a form more readily accessible than that of an
article within the pages of a multi-volume learned
encyclopedia" (ibid., p. 42). It is our aim here to
make accessible such a translation, with notes and
expanded bibliography to serve the general reader.
The importance of the encyclopedia where "Jesus
Christus" originally appeared, something of the author's stance, and a few characteristics of his presentation itself will be sketched in this Introduction, to
undergird the judgment quoted above.

The multivolume series, *Die Religion in Geschichte
und Gegenwart* (commonly referred to as *"RGG"*),
has served for over half a century as the standard

reference work in religion and theology in the German-speaking world. With its origin in the university-academic community, usually involving professors and other experts in Protestant faculties (there is also a Catholic *Lexikon für Theologie und Kirche*), *RGG* has pursued a policy of a new edition every twenty to thirty years. Thus *RGG* first appeared between the years 1909 and 1913. The second edition came out 1927–32. A third edition, from which Conzelmann's article is taken, was somewhat delayed by World War II, but was published in six volumes (plus a supplementary index volume) from 1956 to 1962. New writers are generally appointed for articles in each edition, and it is not simply a matter of revising previous presentations or of updating the bibliography.

So influential have the five huge volumes of the second edition of *RGG* been, for example, that the Yale historian Jaroslav Pelikan has edited a three-volume collection of articles in translation under the significant title of *Twentieth Century Theology in the Making* (New York: Harper & Row; London: Collins, Fontana Books, 1969–70). Pelikan claims that men who "re-drew the theological map" in our century, like Tillich, Barth, and Bultmann, have in their *RGG* articles "set down their thought on the key issues of theology" in a most succinct way (*Twentieth Century Theology in the Making, Vol. I. Themes of Biblical Theology*, trans. R. A. Wilson, p. 14). Accordingly, Professor Pelikan has chosen treatments of biblical theology (by Martin Dibelius), the prophets (by Gunkel and others), eschatology, baptism (Ethelbert Stauffer), and eucharist (Karl Ludwig Schmidt), as well as two by Rudolf Bultmann ("The Gospels [Form]" and "Paul") and the section on "Jesus Christ" as the epoch-making sections on the Bible in

RGG. His other two volumes of selections treat *The Theological Dialogue: Issues and Resources* and *Ecumenicity and Renewal,* and feature material by such giants as Tillich, Friedrich Heiler, Nathan Søderblom, and Adolf von Harnack. Two other articles from *RGG* have also appeared in Facet Books—Biblical Series, published by Fortress Press, Philadelphia. That by Hermann Gunkel on the Psalms, in its two versions in editions one and two of *RGG,* appeared as FBBS 19 (1967), and the treatment on the Lord's Supper in the New Testament by Eduard Schweizer in *RGG* 3d ed., as FBBS 18 (1967) (see note 48, below).

It is natural therefore that, with the publication of the third edition of *RGG,* hope should have arisen for a full and prompt translation of the German encyclopedia in its newest incarnation. For several years plans have been under way for such a version, to be called the *Chicago Encyclopedia of Religion,* under Professor Jerald C. Brauer, to be published by the University of Chicago Press, a project toward which the Evangelical Church in Germany has made a financial contribution. Because of the fact that many articles in *RGG* specialize in continental history and conditions, and other topics of interest in the American scene might well be expanded or added, and because of a desire to recast the *CER* version of *RGG* more along the lines of history-of-religions scholarship, the article on "Jesus Christ" by Conzelmann will not appear in the Chicago publication but can thus appear with a separate identity of its own, such as Professor Perrin hoped for.

Needless to say, the assignment to treat the subject of Jesus Christ in any encyclopedia is a sensitive one. A ranking and mature scholar is needed, but not one who has become identified with some particularly partisan "life" of Jesus or view about him. It is striking that the editors of *RGG* regularly chose an expert well known in New Testament circles but not the author of a biography of Jesus. For the first edition (ed. F. M. Schiele and L. Zscharnack) Wilhelm Heitmüller provided the lengthy treatment on "Jesus Christus" (vol. 3 [1912], cols. 343–410). In *RGG* 2d ed., Karl Ludwig Schmidt, who was known for his pioneer work on form criticism of the New Testament, was the selection (his article is available in translation in *Themes of Biblical Theology* [cited above], pp. 93–168, though without any of the bibliography or cross-references of the original). The choice for the *RGG* article published in 1959 was Hans Conzelmann, known then especially for his work as a redaction critic on Luke-Acts but subsequently emerging as one of the most influential scholars in Germany, a man whose orientation is that of the Bultmann school but who exhibits striking independence of judgment as well as constant theological perception.

Hans Georg Conzelmann was born in Tailfingen, Germany, in 1915. He studied at Tübingen and Marburg, 1934–38. During the war he saw military service and was wounded. Subsequently taking his doctorate at Tübingen (1951), he taught briefly there, at Heidelberg (1952–54), and at Zurich, before becoming professor at Göttingen. His study, *Die Mitte der Zeit,* on how Luke worked as an editor and theologian, is commonly credited with opening the new era of interest in the theologies of the Synoptic evangelists. Over the years Professor Conzelmann has published commentaries on the Pastoral Epistles (a revision of Martin Dibelius's work, recently translated into English in the Hermeneia series), Acts, and 1 Corinthians. His New Testament theology is widely regarded as the standard replacement for Bultmann's textbook in that area. He has also produced a history of primitive Christianity, numerous articles in periodicals and for reference works, and is an editor for *Evangelische Theologie*. For details, see "For Further Reading" at the end of this book, and for the range of his interests in New Testament studies compare some of the footnotes to "Jesus Christ" where other articles of his in *RGG* are noted. A member of the Evangelical Church, Dr. Conzelmann has been a participant in the international Lutheran-Roman Catholic dialogue which completed its work in 1972. He is also of influence through the large number of pupils who have completed doctoral dissertations under him.

The encyclopedia article on "Jesus Christ" thus derives importance from its place of publication, *RGG,* and from the significance of its author, but Professor Conzelmann's stance and certain features of his presentation also help to account for the meaningfulness which Professor Perrin and others see in it. Perrin describes it as "a presentation of the current situation in life of Christ research, as seen from the perspective of the radical acceptance of the form-critical view of the sources characteristic of the Bultmann school" (p. 42). Here is the first factor to be pointed out about the essay itself: Conzelmann not only accepts, he applies the results of the critical-historical approach to the life of Jesus which developed over precisely the period in this century that the three editions of *RGG* cover. Assumed are the general nonhistoricity of the Fourth Gospel, the two-source hypothesis regarding the Synoptics, and thoroughgoing form-critical and redactional assessment of every passage (Conzelmann himself admirably states most of these points in outlining his approach, but to appreciate what is involved one must refer to related *RGG* articles on each point or to their English equivalents).

Secondly, Conzelmann's article can be called a fruit of the new quest of the historical Jesus, for it appeared when in many ways that quest was at its height. It is well known that in the nineteenth century and down to about 1920 both liberals and conservatives engaged in a massive effort to recover what Jesus was like historically, as a base for faith and morals today. Then came the advent of form criticism which, along with other factors, put an end to such a quest. (In some ways, *RGG* 1st ed. reflects the earlier outlook, and *RGG* 2d ed. the newer conditions.) But in 1953 Ernst Käsemann, though a member of the Bultmann school, called for a new quest, for both scholarly and theological reasons, and what is more called for it from within the circle of Bultmann's own pupils (see the literature for Section 12, below, for the title and publication details of Käsemann's address and for other literature on this new quest). In 1956 Günther Bornkamm produced a "life," *Jesus of Nazareth,* which reflected the spirit of this new enterprise (which is really more concerned with Jesus' teachings and view of existence than with his career or biography).

It was in this situation of the new quest that Conzelmann had to write his encyclopedia article. He was generally in sympathy with the quest's intent, and wrote several important articles on aspects of life-of-Jesus study, including its methodology. However, he did not produce a "life" (like those of Bultmann or Bornkamm, other than this article) and soon announced his withdrawal from the quest and, like Käsemann, his dissatisfaction with much that was put forth under the guise of this endeavor. In many ways, however, Conzelmann's "Jesus Christ" represents a highwater mark of the new quest in its general representation of the position of the Bultmann school on the topic.

Thirdly, however, it deserves to be mentioned that, like most Bultmannites, Conzelmann does not follow a narrow party line but exhibits a real independence of outlook. (This is a characteristic of Bultmann's pupils generally.) Thus, while he follows the Bultmannian position on the use of the critical method in Bible study, particularly of form criticism, Conzelmann has his own independent judgments on a number of issues. Thus, for example, he contests the view dear to Bultmann (and classically worked out by H. E. Tödt) that Jesus spoke of someone else as Son of man, a Son-of-man figure whom he expected to come after him; Conzelmann prefers the view that these Son-of-man sayings, like other sayings using the term, are creations of the early church, not statements from the historical Jesus. Similarly with the question of a unity in Jesus' message of eschatology and ethics. While Bultmann stressed this, Conzelmann is more inclined to allow a certain disjointedness of statements, different elements appearing side by side, just as in Jewish tradition.

A final characteristic that I note here has to do with Conzelmann's theological position. Where it emerges, it is an Evangelical (Lutheran Reformation) "theology of the word." Hence the emphasis on preaching (proclamation) as that which contemporizes Jesus for us today.

The translator, Dr. J. Raymond Lord, is professor at the College of Idaho (Caldwell, Idaho). As early as 1967 he suggested the project, which others who knew the *RGG* article heartily endorsed.

The editor is responsible for revising the translation and for most of the notes. In *RGG* articles, bibliographies are given at the end of the entire account, though often numbered by section. We have expanded these lists of titles by giving fuller publication data than in *RGG*, adding reference to English translations where possible, and moving the bibliographies to the beginning of each section. This, in turn, facilitates identification of opinions by scholars on an issue, since they are often referred to in *RGG* simply by the man's name, e.g., "(Bultmann)." Footnotes are not used in *RGG*, but its editors do employ a complex system of cross-references by inserting an arrow into the text before a term on which there is an *RGG* article. We have not followed this system but have incorporated all such cross-references in footnotes where the author's name, article title, and *RGG* volume and columns are cited.

Where Conzelmann gives simply an author's name in the text as the source for a view cited, we have generally footnoted it and added a more precise reference to the book or article involved. Where a footnote is not provided for such a name, the publication involved will usually be found listed under that person's name in the literature for the section. On rare occasions we have provided in a footnote explanatory material for the general reader not found in *RGG*. However the temptation to add titles amplifying or paralleling elsewhere what Conzelmann and *RGG* provide, has generally been resisted. Such additions, where made, are regularly placed in brackets. A limited number of supplementary titles is provided under "For Further Reading" at the end of the book.

John Reumann

Lutheran Theological Seminary, Philadelphia
January 12, 1973

List of Abbreviations

ATANT   Abhandlungen zur Theologie des Alten und Neuen Testaments (Zurich: Zwingli).

BZNW   Beihefte zur Zeitschrift für die neutestamentliche Wissenschaft (Berlin: Töpelmann).

FBBS   Facet Books—Biblical Series (Philadelphia: Fortress).

FRLANT Forschungen zur Religion und Literatur des Alten und Neuen Testaments (Göttingen: Vandenhoeck & Ruprecht).

JBL   *Journal of Biblical Literature.*

RGG   *Die Religion in Geschichte und Gegenwart* (Tübingen: J. C. B. Mohr [Paul Siebeck]). The reference is to the 3d ed. (1956–62), unless otherwise indicated. Cited by volume and column(s), thus: 3: 619–53=vol. 3, cols. 619–53.

SBT   Studies in Biblical Theology (London: SCM; Naperville, Ill.: Allenson).

SNTSMS Society for New Testament Studies Monograph Series (New York: Cambridge University Press). Second series cited thus: 2/6=second series, vol. 6

ThL   *Theologische Literaturzeitung.*

ZNW   *Zeitschrift für die neutestamentliche Wissenschaft.*

ZThK   *Zeitschrift für Theologie und Kirche.*

Motifs in Life-of-Jesus Research

LITERATURE FOR SECTION 1:
The literature is immense. Hence for individual topics reference must be made to other entries where the titles are listed in *RGG:* Vielhauer, Philipp. "Erlöser. II. Im NT." 2: 579–84; Conzelmann, Hans. "Eschatologie. IV. Im Urchristentum." 2: 665–72; Stendahl, Krister. "Kirche. II. Im Urchristentum." 3: 1297–1304; Schreiber, Johannes. "Sohn Gottes. II. Im NT." 6: 119–20; etc.; further, to general references such as: Bornkamm, Günther. "Evangelien, formgeschichtlich." 2: 749–53; ——. "Evangelien, synoptische." 2: 753–66 (with bibliography on the history of interpretation, by Wilfrid Werbeck, 2: 766–69); as well as the pertinent treatments in Walter Bauer's *A Greek-English Lexicon of the New Testament . . .*, trans. and adapted by William F. Arndt and F. Wilbur Gingrich (Chicago: University of Chicago Press, 1957); and in the *Theological Dictionary of the New Testament,* ed. Gerhard Kittel and Gerhard Friedrich, 9 vols. Eng. trans. by G. W. Bromiley in process (Grand Rapids: Eerdmans, 1964–   ).

Older literature is given in the article "Jesus Christ" by Karl Ludwig Schmidt in *RGG* 2d ed. (1927–32), 3: 151; Eng. trans. by R. A. Wilson in *Twentieth Century Theology in the Making,* 3 vols., ed. Jaroslav Pelikan, *Vol. I Themes of Biblical Theology* (London: William Collins; New York: Harper & Row, 1969), pp. 93–168 (bibliography not included in the translation).

Research Reports:

Schweitzer, Albert. *Von Reimarus zu Wrede: Eine Geschichte der Leben-Jesu-Forschung.* Tübingen: Mohr, 1906. Eng. trans. by W. Montgomery, *The Quest of the Historical Jesus: A Critical Study of its Progress from Reimarus to Wrede.* Preface by F. C. Burkitt. London: A. & C. Black, 1910; New York: Macmillan,

1948; paperback, 1961; new paperback ed. with introduction by James M. Robinson, 1968; 2d German ed.,
rev., *Die Geschichte der Leben-Jesu-Forschung.*
Tübingen, 1913; 6th ed. 1951 (never translated).

McCown, Chester Charlton. *The Search for the Real
Jesus: A Century of Historical Study.* The Interna-
tional Library of Christian Knowledge. New York:
Scribner's, 1940.

Hoffmann, Jean G. H. *Les Vies de Jésus et le Jésus de
l'histoire. Étude de la valeur historique des Vies de
Jésus de langue française, non catholiques, d'Ernest
Renan à Charles Guignebert.* Acta Seminarii Neotesta-
mentici Upsaliensis 17. Lund: Gleerups; Copenhagen:
Munksgaard; Paris: Messageries evangéliques, 1947.

Veit, M. "Die Auffassung von der Person Jesu im Urchristentum nach den neuesten Forschungen." Dissertation, Marburg, 1949.

Piper, Otto A. "Das Problem des Lebens Jesu seit
Schweitzer." In *Verbum Dei Manet in Aeternum:
Festschrift für Otto Schmitz.* Ed. Werner Foerster.
Witten: Luther-Verlag, 1953. Pp. 73–93.

Manson, T. W. "The Life of Jesus: Some Tendencies in
Present-day Research." In *The Background of the New
Testament and Its Eschatology: In Honour of Charles
Harold Dodd,* ed. W. D. Davies and D. Daube. New
York: Cambridge University Press, 1954; reprinted
1964. Pp. 211–21.

Kümmel, W. G. *Das Neue Testament: Geschichte der
Erforschung seiner Probleme.* Freiburg: Verlag Karl
Alber, 1958. Eng. trans. by S. MacLean Gilmour and
Howard Clark Kee, *The New Testament: The History
of the Investigation of Its Problems.* New York &
Nashville: Abingdon, 1972.

General Presentations:

Klausner, Joseph. *Jesus of Nazareth: His Life, Times,
and Teaching.* Trans. from the Hebrew by Herbert
Danby. New York: Macmillan, 1925; paperback reprint, Boston: Beacon Press, 1964.

Bultmann, Rudolf. *Jesus.* Berlin: Deutsche Bibliothek,
1926. Eng. trans. by Louise Pettibone Smith and Er-

2

minie Huntress, *Jesus and the Word*. New York: Scribner's, 1934.

Feine, Paul. *Jesus*. Gütersloh: Bertelsmann, 1930.

Easton, Burton Scott. *Christ in the Gospels*. New York: Scribner's, 1930.

————. *What Jesus Taught: The Sayings Translated and Arranged with Expository Commentary*. New York: Abingdon, 1938.

Mackinnon, James. *The Historic Jesus*. London: Longmans, 1931.

Braun, François Marie. *Où en est le problème de Jésus?* Brussels: Editions de la Cité chrétienne; Paris: Gabalda, 1932.

Goguel, Maurice. *La Vie de Jésus*. Paris: Payot, 1932. Eng. trans. by Olive Wyon, *The Life of Jesus*. New York: Macmillan, 1933. Reprinted as *Jesus and the Origins of Christianity*, paperback in 2 vols. New York: Harper Torchbooks, 1960, with an introduction by C. Leslie Mitton.

Burkitt, F. C. *Jesus Christ: an Historical Outline*. London & Glasgow: Blackie & Son, 1932.

Prat, Ferdinand, S. J. *Jésus-Christ, sa vie, sa doctrine, son oeuvre*. 2 vols. Paris: Beauchesne, 1933. Eng. trans. by John J. Heenan, S. J., *Jesus Christ: His Life, His Teaching, and His Work*. Milwaukee: Bruce Publishing Company, 1950, 2 vols. in one.

Adam, Karl. *Jesus Christus*. Augsburg: Haas & Brabherr, 1933.

Otto, Rudolf. *Reich Gottes und Menschensohn*. Munich: Beck, 1934; 3d. ed. 1954. Eng. trans. from the rev. German ed. by Floyd V. Filson and Bertram Lee Woolf, *The Kingdom of God and the Son of Man: A Study in the History of Religion*. Lutterworth Library, 9. London: Lutterworth, 1938; rev. ed., 1943.

Dibelius, Martin. *Jesus*. Berlin: de Gruyter, 1939; 2d ed. 1949. Eng. trans. by Charles B. Hedrick and F. C. Grant, *Jesus*. Philadelphia: Westminster, 1949.

Cadoux, C. J. *The Historic Mission of Jesus: A Constructive Reexamination of the Eschatological Teaching in the Synoptic Gospels*. London: Lutterworth; New York: Harper, 1941.

————. *The Life of Jesus*. West Drayton, Middlesex: Penguin Books, 1948 (Pelican Books A189).

Grønbeck, Vilhelm Peter. *Jesus, Menneskesønnen*. Copenhagen: P. Branner, 1944.

Rawlinson, A. E. J. *Christ in the Gospels*. New York: Oxford, 1944.

Bowman, John Wick. *The Intention of Jesus*. Philadelphia: Westminster, 1945.

Manson, William. *Jesus the Messiah: The Synoptic Tradition of the Revelation of God in Christ: With Special Reference to Form-Criticism*. Philadelphia: Westminster, 1946. German trans., *Bist Du der da kommen soll?* 1952.

Cadbury, Henry J. *Jesus What Manner of Man?* New York: Macmillan, 1947. Paperback ed., London: SPCK, 1962.

Büchsel, Friedrich, *Jesus, Verkündigung und Geschichte*. Gütersloh: Bertelsmann, 1947.

Duncan, G. S. *Jesus, Son of Man: Studies Contributory to a Modern Portrait*. London: Nisbet & Co., 1947.

Goodspeed, E. J. *A Life of Jesus*. New York: Harper, 1950.

Fuller, Reginald H. *The Mission and Achievement of Jesus*. Studies in Biblical Theology, 12. London: SCM; Naperville: Allenson, 1954.

Taylor, Vincent. *The Life and Ministry of Jesus*. New York & Nashville: Abingdon, 1955; paperback reprint 1968.

Bundy, Walter Ernest. *Jesus and the First Three Gospels: An Introduction to the Synoptic Tradition*. Cambridge: Harvard University Press, 1955.

Bornkamm, Günther. *Jesus von Nazareth*. Urban Bücher. Stuttgart: Kohlhammer, 1956, ⁸1969. Eng. trans. by Irene and Fraser McLuskey with James M. Robinson, *Jesus of Nazareth*. New York: Harper, 1960.

Church, L. F. *The Life of Jesus: His Journeying and His Triumph*. London: Epworth, 1956.

Grundmann, Walter. *Die Geschichte Jesu Christi*. Berlin: Evangelische Verlagsanstalt,1957.

Stauffer, Ethelbert. *Jesus Gestalt und Geschichte*. Dalp Taschenbücher. Bern: Francke Verlag, 1957. Eng. trans. by Dorothea M. Barton, *Jesus and His Story*.

London: SCM, 1960. American trans. by Richard and Clara Winston, *Jesus and His Story*. New York: Knopf, 1960.

THE HISTORICAL and substantive presupposition for modern research into the life of Jesus is emancipation from traditional christological dogma on the basis of the principle of reason. The decisive impulse was given by David Friedrich Strauss.[1]

While it is true that Strauss himself did not undertake any methodological source criticism, nevertheless as a result of his work source analysis became unavoidable. Already during the nineteenth century certain foundations were laid which remain valid to the present time. Among these was the realization that the starting point for historical reconstruction of the life of Jesus must be the Synoptic presentation rather than the Johannine.[2] The interrelationship of the Synoptics was clarified through the "two-source hypothesis." According to this theory, the Gospel of Mark is the oldest of the Synoptics and is a source for both of the others. In addition, there is a second source called Q (*Quelle*), used by Matthew and Luke. On the basis of this hypothesis it was hoped that the life of Jesus and his historical figure could be traced by gaining the sketch of his ministry from Mark and the outline of his teaching from Mark and Q.

Around the turn of the century a certain consensus was reached concerning the approach (not, of course, without protest—notably that of Martin Kähler[3]): investigation sought after the *personality* of Jesus,

1. E. Schott, "Strauss, David Friedrich," *RGG* 6: 416–17.
2. G. Bornkamm, "Evangelien, synoptische," *RGG* 2: 753–66; R. Bultmann, "Johannesevangelium," ibid. 3: 840–50.
3. R. Hermann, "Kähler, Martin," *RGG* 3: 1081–84. [Cf. *The So-Called Historical Jesus and the Historic, Biblical Christ*, trans. and ed. Carl E. Braaten, Seminar Editions (Philadelphia: Fortress, 1964).]

5

after the enduring religious and ethical content of his teaching. There was the conviction that the historical reconstruction could be the basis for a contemporary philosophy of life. In this reconstruction scholars projected a great deal of their own conception of the "essence of Christianity"[4] into the teaching of Jesus. For example, Jesus was understood as the teacher and model of genuine humanity. Whenever the kingdom of God[5] could not be interpreted in the sense of a timeless ideal, the eschatological proclamation was devaluated as being merely conditioned by Jesus' own times. Gaps in the preserved records were filled in through psychological conjectures. The story of the baptism of Jesus was interpreted as the experience of a divine call, that of the temptation as a process of inward clarification of this experience. Scholars distinguished stages of inner and outer development: the first successes in Galilee; the gathering of the crowds; then their turning away; the crisis which brought about Jesus' decision to go up to Jerusalem after the disciples had come to believe in him as the messiah; and finally the catastrophe.

The History-of-Religions School[6] protested against all tendencies to modernize the ideas of Jesus. This school described these ideas precisely as conditioned by his own time and laid stress on the central significance of eschatology in his thought (Johannes Weiss, Albert Schweitzer).[7] It is impossible to under-

4. [The phrase "Wesen des Christentums" alludes to a lecture series in 1899–1900 by Adolf von Harnack; Eng. trans. by T. B. Saunders, *What Is Christianity?* (New York: Putnam's, 1901, often reprinted).]
5. Ernst Wolf, "Reich Gottes. II. Theologiegeschichtlich," *RGG* 5: 918–24, especially 921–23.

6. J. Hempel, "Religionsgeschichtliche Schule," *RGG* 5: 991–94.
7. H. Conzelmann, "Eschatologie. IV. Im Urchristentum. 3. Jesus," *RGG* 2: 666–68. W. G. Kümmel, "Weiss, Johannes," *RGG* 6: 1582–83. R. Grabs, "Schweitzer, Albert," *RGG* 5: 1607–1608. [Cf. Johannes Weiss, *Jesus' Proclamation of the Kingdom of God*, trans. R. H. Hiers and D. L. Holland from German 1st ed. (1892), Lives of

stand the kingdom of God merely as "an inward kingdom of transformed minds" ("inneres Reich der Sinnesänderung"). In Jesus' opinion it would break in as a cosmic catastrophe in the immediate future. Such an emphasis also led to a new approach in posing the question of Jesus' self-understanding as well as to asking anew about the possible relevance of his statements for the present time.

At the same time that the motif research of the History-of-Religions School was progressing, so also was source analysis. It was recognized with increasing clarity that the gospels are not historical reports, but documents of faith. William Wrede[8] recognized the "messianic secret" as the theology of the primitive church (Gemeindetheologie). According to Wrede, the historical Jesus did not understand himself to be a messiah; therefore, the original tradition did not yet have any messianic character. The early church, which believed in his messiahship on the basis of the Easter experience,[9] reconciled the contradiction between their faith and what they found in the tradition by means of this theory of the "messianic secret": i.e., that Jesus knew himself to be the messiah, but he kept it secret. This raised the question of the relationship between the genuine teaching of Jesus and the christological statements of the post-Easter church.

Jesus Series (Philadelphia: Fortress, 1971). In addition to Schweitzer's *Quest of the Historical Jesus*, see the Eng. trans. by Walter Lowrie of Schweitzer's 1901 book, *The Mystery of the Kingdom of God: The Secret of Jesus' Messiahship and Passion* (New York: Macmillan, 1950).]

8. G. Strecker, "Wrede, William," *RGG* 6: 1821–22. W. Wrede, *Das Messiasgeheimnis in den Evangelien: Zugleich ein Beitrag zum Verständnis des Markusevangeliums* (Göttingen: Vandenhoeck & Ruprecht, 1901, 2d ed. 1913); Eng. trans. by J. C. G. Greig, *The Messianic Secret*, The Library of Theological Translations, ed. William Barclay (Cambridge & London: James Clarke & Co., 1971).

9. H. Conzelmann, "Auferstehung Christi. I. Im NT," *RGG* 1: 698–700.

The confidence of the "liberals" yielded to the skepticism of the "historians of religion."

An additional step was taken when this skepticism was applied methodologically, when scholars sought by methodical analysis to determine the contribution of the early church to the formation of the gospels. This took place through form criticism (Karl Ludwig Schmidt, Martin Dibelius, Rudolf Bultmann).[10] The "framework of the history of Jesus"[11] was shown to be secondary, literary redaction. Thus it was no longer possible to discover the sequence of events in the life of Jesus, to write a biography of him, or to sketch his portrait. Depending upon one's point of view, the results of form criticism were regarded as a destruction or a liberation. Both liberal and conservative "life-of-Jesus theology" viewed it as the former; dialectical theology saw it as the latter, in the sense that now, in the place of the "historical Jesus," the "Christ of faith" had become evident. According to dialectical theology, the "christological witness" (Christuszeugnis) of the gospels now appeared all the more clearly since they were no longer exploited primarily as historical sources.

Naturally the systematic problem of the "historical Jesus" was not settled through the fact that the source material was reduced to a minimum. The problem

10. G. Bornkamm, "Evangelien, formgeschichtlich," *RGG* 2: 749–53. O. Cullmann, "Schmidt, Karl Ludwig," *RGG* 5: 1458. W. G. Kümmel, "Dibelius, Martin," *RGG* 2: 181. E. Fuchs, "Bultmann, Rudolf," *RGG* 1: 1511–12. See also Section 2, below, on form-critical treatment of the gospels. [K. L. Schmidt, *Der Rahmen der Geschichte Jesu: Literarkritische Untersuchungen zur ältesten Jesusüberlieferung* (Berlin: Trowitzsch und Sohn, 1919; reprinted Darmstadt: Wissenschaftliche Buchgesellschaft, 1969; no Eng. trans.). Dibelius's 1919 volume is translated by Bertram Lee Woolf as *From Tradition to Gospel* (New York: Scribner's, 1935, paperback reprint 1965). Bultmann's 1921 volume finally appeared in Eng., trans. John Marsh, as *The History of the Synoptic Tradition* (New York: Harper & Row, 1963).]
11. [The phrase alludes to the title of K. L. Schmidt's book in 1919, cited above, note 10.]

had to return at some time, even if, for the time being, it had been relegated to the background. It was indeed significant that each of the three leading form critics wrote a life of Jesus.[12]

To be sure, the form-critical method was only partially accepted. Outside of Germany it was largely dismissed or limited to a formal classification of materials from the tradition (thus understood non-historically, as, e.g., with Vincent Taylor[13]). It was denied that this method could be used to determine whether a tradition was historically genuine or not. The historicity of the Markan outline was generally retained, as well as the historical character of the messianic secret. Because of the impression that form criticism had led into a blind alley or into excessive resignation, some scholars tried anew to arrive at a constructive-synthetic account. Rudolf Otto[14] believed that he could discover the structure of Jesus' self-understanding by the motif-research of the History-of-Religions School. Similar attempts were made by the school of "realized eschatology" (C. H. Dodd, William Manson, T. W. Manson), starting from a new overall understanding of the message of the kingdom of God.[15]

---

12. C. H. Ratschow, "Jesusbild der Gegenwart," *RGG* 3: 655–63. For K. L. Schmidt, see *RGG* 2d ed. (1927–32), 3: 110 ff., Eng. trans. in *Twentieth Century Theology in the Making* (cited in the literature for Section 1), 1: 93–168. Bultmann's *Jesus* (1926) and Dibelius's *Jesus* (1939) are also listed, including Eng. trans., in the same bibliography.

13. [Cf. Taylor's lectures from 1932, *The Formation of the Gospel Tradition* (London: Macmillan, 1933, 2d ed. 1935).]

14. G. Wünsch, "Otto, Rudolf," *RGG* 4: 1749–50. [Cf. Otto's book (1934), *The Kingdom of God and the Son of Man: A Study in the History of Religion*, trans. F. V. Filson and B. Lee Woolf (London: Lutterworth, 1938; rev. ed. 1943).]

15. J. Jeremias, "Dodd, Charles Harold," *RGG* 2: 214–15. K. Grobel, "Manson, Thomas Walter," *RGG* 4: 727. [Cf. Dodd's *Parables of the Kingdom* (London: Nisbet, 1935) and *The Apostolic Preaching and its Developments* (London: Hodder & Stoughton, 1936; further, *The Coming of Christ* (New York: Cambridge University Press, 1951) and *The Founder of Christianity* (London: Macmillan, 1970). Wil-

Apparently scholars were, for the time being, coming to a far-reaching, international consensus, namely, that Jesus understood himself in the sense of a combination of the Son-of-man and Servant-of-God ideas, and that he connected these concepts with the idea of the kingdom of God and linked them to his own person. This explains not only his tie with Jewish messianic tradition, but also the specifically new element in his sayings and his use of traditional concepts. From this self-understanding one could also understand his self-veiling (i.e., the messianic secret, which now again was recognized as a historical fact), as well as his awareness of being destined to suffer, and also the form and content of his ethics. Finally one was also able to bridge the gap which form criticism had opened—viz., that between the teaching of Jesus and the faith of the primitive church. Form criticism had been unable to show any other link than the Easter experience of the disciples. The new hypothesis believed it was able to show that the faith[16] of the early church, in its essence, specifically in its interpretation of the person of Jesus, went back to Jesus himself. This provided historical continuity. The great impasse of previous life-of-Jesus research was overcome.

As a result of all this, one gets the impression that scholarly research has finally come full circle and returned again to its point of departure: the messianic portrait of dogmatics seems in its essential features to be traced back to Jesus himself. Faith thereby appears to have gained a historical foundation. However,

---

liam Manson, *Jesus the Messiah* (cited in the literature for Section 1). For T. W. Manson, see his essay cited under "Research Reports," literature for Section 1, and *The Servant-Messiah: A Study of the Public Ministry of Jesus* (New York: Cambridge University Press, 1953, often reprinted, paperback 1961), which well illustrates the "international consensus" to which the next paragraph refers.]
16. H. Braun, "Glaube. III. Im NT," *RGG* 2: 1590–97.

quite apart from the systematic question of whether the relation of faith to history has been rightly understood, there remains the historical question of whether this new picture of Jesus can be verified by the sources and also whether it can be justified methodologically over against form criticism. Until now such attempts (e.g., that by William Manson[17]) have not been convincing. One becomes suspicious when it is necessary to postulate unknown factors (e.g., esoteric instruction to the disciples) and to construct the overall picture of the self-understanding of Jesus with the aid of psychological considerations or through the assumption of a development on his part after all. With that, one is going beyond the sources. What, then, do these sources yield?

17. *Jesus the Messiah* (cited in the literature for Section 1).

The Sources

LITERATURE FOR SECTION 2:

Compare the literature cited by W. Foerster, "Josephus, Flavius," *RGG* 3: 869, as well as Klausner, *Jesus of Nazareth,* and Goguel, *Jesus and the Origins of Christianity* (cited above, under "General Presentations," literature for Section 1). Further:

Windisch, Hans. "Das Problem der Geschichtlichkeit Jesu." *Theologische Rundschau* NF 1 (1929): 266–88.

Jeremias, Joachim. *Unbekannte Jesuworte.* Beiträge zur Förderung christlicher Theologie, 45, 2. Gütersloh: Bertelsmann, 1948; 2d ed. 1951; 3d ed., with O. Hofius, Gütersloh: Gerd Mohn, 1963. Eng. trans. by Reginald Fuller, *Unknown Sayings of Jesus.* London: SPCK, 1952; 2d ed. 1964.

——. "Kennzeichen der ipsissima vox Jesu." *Synoptische Studien: Alfred Wikenhauser zum siebzigsten Geburtstag am 22. Februar 1953.* . . . Munich: Zink, 1953. Pp. 86–93. Eng. trans. by John Bowden, "Characteristics of the ipsissima vox Jesu," in *The Prayers of Jesus,* SBT 2/6 (1967). Pp. 108–15.

Grant, F. C. "The Authenticity of Jesus' Sayings." *Neutestamentliche Studien für Rudolf Bultmann zu seinem siebzigsten Geburtstag am 20. August 1954.* BZNW 21. Berlin: Töpelmann, 1954. Pp. 137–43.

Köster, Helmut. "Die ausserkanonische Herrenworte als Produkte der christlichen Gemeinde." *ZNW* 48 (1957): 220–37.

In general, see the commentaries and Bultmann, *History of the Synoptic Tradition* (cited above, note 10), particularly the literature in the Supplement.

THE NON-CHRISTIAN source material is extremely scanty.[18] It confirms the fact that there was never

18. Presented in Klausner, *Jesus of Nazareth* (cited under "General Presentations," literature for Section 1), pp. 17 ff.; and in Goguel,

any doubt about the historicity of the person Jesus, but it yields nothing of concrete knowledge about him. The material is divided into two groups: references to Jesus in ancient historians, and references in the talmudic literature.

(a) In the report of the burning of Rome (under Nero), Tacitus (*Annals* 15. 44) mentions the persecution of Christians[19] which was caused in connection with it and remarks there that this "name," this "awful superstition," goes back to "Christus," who had been sentenced to death under Pontius Pilate. This is nothing more than one could discover anywhere in Rome. Tacitus has only a very vague notion of the spread of Christianity. He considers, as does Pliny the Younger and evidently the entire Roman public, "Christus" to be a proper name.

It is uncertain whether the notice in Suetonius (*Claudius* 25. 4) refers to Jesus: "Claudius expelled the Jews from Rome because in his reign, upon the instigation of a certain Chrestus, riots had broken out." Do we have here confused information about the penetration of Christianity into Rome? In any case, Suetonius knows nothing precise; he is apparently of the opinion that this Chrestus had personally appeared in the city.

More significant are two passages in Josephus[20]: *Antiquities* 18. 63–64 (18. 3.3); 20. 200 (20.9.1). The first passage (the so-called "Testimonium Flavianum") is, in its present form at least, a Christian interpolation. It is generally accepted that there is present as a minimum an authentic core in this passage. Against this view is the fact, not hitherto ap-

Jesus and the Origins of Christianity (cited under "General Presentations"), 1: 70–104.

19. K. Wessel, "Christenverfolgungen," *RGG* 1: 1730–32.

20. W. Foerster, "Josephus," *RGG* 3: 868–69.

preciated, that the passage is constructed in accord with a pattern of the Christian kerygma (and indeed the Lukan one). One must therefore conclude that the passage *as a whole* has been interpolated. On the other hand, *Antiquities* 20. 200 does go back to Josephus. The passage is about the execution of James[21] in A. D. 62; he is introduced as the brother of Jesus: *ton adelphon Iēsou tou legomenou Christou,* "the brother of Jesus who was called Christ." Here Josephus designates Jesus by the "name" under which he was known to his Roman audience.

The often-mentioned Thallus cannot be considered as a witness.[22] Likewise a few bits of inscriptional evidence—the "Diatagma Kaisaros" and the ossuaries from Jerusalem on which the name "Jesus" occurs— must be rejected as sources.[23]

(b) The content of the most important references to Jesus in the Talmud amounts to roughly the following:[24] Jesus of Nazareth engaged in sorcery; he led Israel astray; he mocked the words of the wise, had five (!) disciples; he was hanged on the eve of the Passover (b Sanh. 43a); he was an illegitimate child of a Roman soldier named Panthera. Of value here is simply the fact that the existence of Jesus is nowhere called into question. The fact that his miracles are not disputed does not mean anything, considering the nature of these texts.

Among the Christian sources outside the gospels there are, first of all, the widely circulated kerygmatic

21. K. Aland, "Jakobus, Bruder Jesu," *RGG* 3: 525–26.

22. *Die Fragmente der griechischen Historiker,* ed. F. Jacoby (Berlin: Weidmann, 1923–30), No. 256; texts in *Zweiter Teil, Zeitgeschichte,* B., Dritte Lieferung (1929), pp. 1156–58, with discussion in *Zweiter Teil,* D. (1930), pp. 835–37.

23. H. Braun, "Christentum. I. Entstehung, 2. Jesus von Nazareth," *RGG* 1: 1686–88.

24. Klausner, *Jesus of Nazareth* (cited under "General Presentations," literature for Section 1), pp. 18–54.

formulas mentioning the death of Jesus,[25] and the *agrapha*[26] or detached sayings of Jesus. In any case, we gain nothing substantial for understanding the teaching of Jesus from the *agrapha,* particularly since authenticity cannot be proved in any instance (contrary to the view of Joachim Jeremias).[27] Thus there remain the four canonical gospels, and again among these it is essentially the Synoptics, the interrelationship among which is made clear through the "two-source hypothesis" (see Section 1). In evaluating these, the fact that the chronological and geographical plan of the Gospel of Mark is not ancient tradition, but literary redaction—a fact recognized through form criticism—must be taken into consideration.[28] Thus only the individual traditions which have been built into the present literary framework can be used as primary sources. Even among these, authenticity must be questioned from case to case. In particular, some of the narratives' "ideal scenes" do not represent historical events (Bultmann).[29] This means that for a great portion of the tradition there is no possibility of establishing the exact place in the life of Jesus. We no longer know the sequence of events and, above all, we cannot reconstruct an outer and inner development.

Not only are the gospels in their entirety witnesses of faith, but this is true already of the individual pieces of tradition. For that reason they have no interest in the "portrait" of Jesus. One discovers

25. G. Bornkamm, "Formen. II. Im Neuen Testament, 2a. Glaubensformeln," *RGG,* 2: 1002–1003.

26. J. Jeremias, "Agrapha," *RGG* 1: 177–78.

27. [Cf. J. Jeremias, *Unknown Sayings of Jesus* (cited in the literature for Section 2).]

28. G. Bornkamm, "Evangelien, formgeschichtlich. 2. Formen und Geschichte der Tradition," *RGG* 2: 750–53.

29. *History of the Synoptic Tradition* (cited above, note 10), pp. 56 ff. and passim.

nothing about his appearance, his human character, his habits, nothing about the commonplace things in his life. Insight into this character of the tradition prevents psychological-biographical evaluation of a great part of the material. This applies especially to the epiphany stories (baptism, transfiguration). The reports of these reveal absolutely nothing about inner experiences of Jesus; they are constructed from the post-Easter perspective of the church's faith. The same is true about the prophecies of his "passion." They do not represent a clear-sighted judgment of the situation; rather they are dogmatic assertions about the necessity of the passion as this was conceived by the church after his death.

What, then, can be regarded as authentic (in the sense of historical "fact")? No methodological guarantee can be acquired in a particular case. Nevertheless we do possess a few solid footholds. To these belong, among the events, a series of scenes whose genuineness cannot be contested. Above all this is true of the core of the passion story (see Section 11). For the reconstruction of Jesus' teaching (see Section 10), the following methodological principle is valid: whatever fits neither into Jewish thought nor the views of the later church can be regarded as authentic. This is the case, above all, for the sayings which express a consciousness of the uniqueness of his own situation. To this principle one can add certain observations about form. Such observations guarantee above all the genuineness of the core of the parables.[30] These are clearly distinguished from all Jewish parallels through style (narrative form, imagery) as well as thought, and reflect a sharply defined self-understanding in which teaching and action (miracle) are comprehended as an indissoluble unity.

30. N. A. Dahl, "Gleichnis und Parabel. II. In der Bibel. 3. Im Neuen Testament," *RGG* 2: 1617–19.

3

The World of the Day

LITERATURE FOR SECTION 3:

Besides the literature on Qumran listed by M. Burrows, R. de Vaux, R. Meyer, K. G. Kuhn, and C.-H. Hunzinger in *RGG* 5: 740–56, see:

Olmstead, A. T. *Jesus in the Light of History.* New York: Scribner's, 1942.

Birkeland, Harris. *The Language of Jesus.* Skrifter utgitt av Det Norske Videnskaps-Akademi i Oslo 2, Historisk-filosofisk Klasse, 1954, no. 1. Oslo: Dybwad, 1954.

Johnson, Sherman E. *Jesus in His Homeland.* New York: Scribner's, 1957.

Schürmann, Heinz. "Die Sprache des Christus." *Biblische Zeitschrift* NF 2 (1958): 54–84.

JESUS MOVED almost exclusively within the framework of Palestinian Judaism.[31] Although Palestine was surrounded by and dotted with Hellenistic cities, these cities have left no mark on the gospels. Sepphoris, which was only a few miles distant from Jesus' home at Nazareth,[32] is not mentioned once. In the oldest stratum of the Synoptic tradition one observes no influence from Hellenistic ideas (its philosophical world view, concept of nature, ethics/moral philosophy, etc.). Jesus acquires the material of his parables from the Jewish milieu. His education is exclusively Jewish; his mother tongue is Aramaic.[33] Political relationships (Rome, the publicans) are seen from the Jewish perspective, but they are not important in

31. K. Galling, "Judentum. I. Vom Exil bis Hadrian," *RGG* 3: 978–86.
32. E. Lohse, "Nazareth," *RGG* 4: 1388.
33. W. Baumgartner, "Aramäisches in der Bibel. II. Im Neuen Testament," *RGG* 1: 534.

themselves. Where the political theme does emerge, it is immediately dismissed as a problem (the saying about the "tribute money," Mark 12:13–17). Comment about the rulers is only marginal until they become involved in Jesus' own life as actors in the passion.

The Jews did not recognize Jesus' home district, Galilee,[34] as completely orthodox. Later tradition made use of this disdain as a motif around which to present the paradoxical character of the divine revelation (Matt. 4:12 ff.). The district had become, since the first deportations by the Assyrians, largely controlled by foreigners and foreign investments. Still, however, in its rural core Galilee may have always remained predominately Jewish.[35] It was re-Judaized by the Maccabees. In Josephus it appears as a center of political activity (Judas the Galilean). Jesus' teaching, however, does not deduce anything causal from the economic (*latifundia*)[36] and political relationships there. When in his parables he takes up images from economic life, it happens without a polemic note.

The religious thinking of contemporary Judaism was dominated by the problems of law and eschatology.[37] The picture has been recently enriched through the discoveries at Qumran.[38] Especially significant is the "heightening of the torah" (in Herbert Braun's phrase) in the Qumran community,[39] which was com-

---

34. H. W. Hertzberg, "Galiläa," *RGG* 2: 1191.

35. Albrecht Alt, "Die Stätten des Wirkens Jesu in Galiläa . . . ," Eng. trans. *Where Jesus Worked* (cited below, in the supplementary bibliography "For Further Reading," in the literature for Section 6).

36. [Latin, the large landed estates, often owned by absentee landlords.]

37. E. Lohse, "Gesetz. III. Im Judentum," *RGG* 2: 1515–17. R. Meyer, "Eschatologie. III. Im Judentum," ibid. 2: 662–65.

38. M. Burrows et al., "Qumran," *RGG* 5: 740–56, especially col. 746 (K. G. Kuhn).

39. H. Braun, *Spätjüdisch-häretischer und frühchristlicher Radikalismus: Jesus von Nazareth und die essenische Qumransekte,*

bined with eschatological urgency, its detachment from the temple cult, the idea of the new covenant and the true eschatological people of God, and community life which expressed itself in communal meals. There are, of course, also differences, which have already been noted: with Jesus, obedience was not just a matter of regulated observance; the Qumran people separated themselves visibly from sinners and taught hate against the "children of darkness"; Jesus turned to sinners. The Qumran people represent the eschatological people of God as being *directly* in their group. Jesus' view is the exact opposite. Membership in the people of God is not organized. It was accomplished simply through repentance and is finally brought to light at the last judgment.

A special problem is the relationship of John the Baptist[40] to the group at Qumran. Their geographical proximity (the wilderness/Jordan) is in itself striking. Further, John radicalized the notion of obedience. This he motivated by imminent eschatological expectation, and called Israel to repentance. But he founded no organization to confer a sense of salvation. He practiced asceticism,[41] but did not make it a condition of salvation. In the place of constant ritual purification he put a single baptism.[42] Jesus could make connection with these negative emphases. In the preaching of the Baptist the farthest limit of Jewish possibilities was reached, and Jesus is conscious of this (Matt. 11:7 ff.; cf. Luke 16:16). Precisely at this point he himself enters upon the scene.

Beiträge zur historischen Theologie 24, 2 vols. (Tübingen: Mohr, 1957), vol. 2, pp. 29 ff., especially 29, 34, 53, 61, 62, and passim.
40. P. Vielhauer, "Johannes, der Täufer," *RGG* 3: 804–808.
41. K. G. Kuhn, "Askese. IV. Im Urchristentum, 1. Johannes der Täufer," *RGG* 1: 642–43.
42. Erich Dinkler, "Taufe. II. Im Urchristentum," *RGG* 6: 627–37, especially col. 628.

4

Chronology

LITERATURE FOR SECTION 4:

Holzmeister, Urban. *Chronologia vitae Christi*. Rome: Pontifical Biblical Institute, 1933.

Jeremias, Joachim. *Die Abendmahlsworte Jesu*. Göttingen: Vandenhoeck & Ruprecht, 1935; ²1949, pp. 10 ff.; ³1959. Eng. trans. by Norman Perrin, *The Eucharistic Words of Jesus*. London: SCM; New York: Scribner's, 1966. Pp. 16 ff.

Lohmeyer, Ernst. "Der Stern der Weisen." *Theologische Blätter* 17 (1938): 289–99.

Ogg, George. *The Chronology of the Public Ministry of Jesus*. New York: Cambridge University Press, 1940.

Steinmetzer, F. X. "Census." In *Reallexikon für Antike und Christentum,* ed. Theodor Klauser. Stuttgart: Hiersemann Verlag. Vol. 2 (1954), pp. 969–72.

Instinsky, Hans Ulrich. *Das Jahr der Geburt Christi: Eine geschichtswissenschaftliche Studie*. Munich: Kösel-Verlag, 1957.

Braunert, Horst. "Der römische Provinzialzensus und der Schätzungsbericht des Lukas-Evangeliums." *Historia* 6 (1957): 192–214.

Blinzler, Josef. "Qumran-Kalendar und Passionschronologie." *ZNW* 49 (1958): 238–51.

Walter, J. A. "The Chronology of the Passion Week." *JBL* 77 (1958): 116–22.

THE GOSPELS present only one single direct chronological statement: according to Luke 3:1–2, John the Baptist appeared in the fifteenth year of the reign of the Emperor Tiberius, i.e., probably A. D. 28 (so E. Stauffer).[43] But we do not know how Luke arrives

---

43. Ethelbert Stauffer, "Münzprägung und Judenpolitik des Pilatus," paper given in the New Testament section of the "Deutscher evangelischer Theologentag zu Marburg" in 1950, reported by K. G. Kuhn, *ThL* 75 (1950), col. 226.

at this date; is it through his own calculation or from a source? The synchronization in which the statement stands is, moreover, laden with inconsistencies. Further, it is not clear what the time period is between the appearance of the Baptist and that of Jesus. Luke, of course, obviously regards it as brief; indeed, he wishes to fix Jesus' own appearance with this date (so Goguel). If, then, the precise year remains uncertain, still the approximate time reference is given correctly, for the date does tally with the assertions about other persons. We know the period of the reign of Herod the Great[44] (until 4 B.C.) and of his sons, Archelaus (until A. D. 6); Herod Antipas, Jesus' ruler (until A. D. 39; cf. Luke 13:31 ff.; 23:6 ff.); and Philip (until A. D. 34; cf. Mark 6:17, where, admittedly, there is some underlying confusion). Pilate[45] was governor A. D. 26–36. The synchronization mentioned above and also the passion narrative name the high priests Annas (A. D. 6–15, also influential after that time) and Caiaphas (A. D. 18–36).[46]

As a result of the poverty of the chronological statements and the lack of any temporal arrangement of the traditional material, we do not know the length of Jesus' public ministry. The Gospel of John knows of three Passovers (John 2:13, 23; 6:4; 11:55; the feast at 5:1 which is not more fully identified is identical with the Passover of 6:4, since chapters 5 and 6 should be transposed). Beyond this, John mentions one feast of Tabernacles (7:2) and one feast of the Dedication (10:22). John thus thinks of a time span of more than two full years. Over against this, the Synoptics know

44. W. Foerster, "Herodes der Grosse," *RGG* 3: 266–68.
45. E. Bammel, "Pilatus," *RGG* 5: 383–84.
46. J. Jeremias, "Hannas," *RGG* 3: 66; E. Bammel, "Kaiphas," ibid. 3: 1091.

only of the one Passover when Jesus died and give no clues for calculating the preceding period of time.

In favor of the Johannine dating one could cite the fact that the Markan dating is obviously connected with the strict geographical schematization of his book, which in turn symbolizes a theological fact (so Ernst Lohmeyer): Galilee is the humble land of eschatological promise, but Jerusalem is the place of hostility.[47] Such a scheme does not permit Jesus to appear in this city until immediately before his death. This observation, of course, does not prove the accuracy of the Johannine chronology, and one should be cautious when he realizes that the statements about the Passover feasts are completely redactional and belong to the latest stratum of the book. One may ask whether in the Gospel of John there is not also reflected a source which reckons in terms of a *one*-year time span.

In the same way observations on individual sayings—for example that perhaps the episode about plucking ears of grain before the harvest in Mark 2:23–28 must assume a time approximately around Passover—lead no further. The saying in Matthew 23:37/Luke 13:34 ("Jerusalem, . . . how often would I have gathered together your children . . .") appears to intimate that Jesus had appeared in Jerusalem several times—contrary to the Synoptic representation. It could, however, be interpreted also as referring to a single, longer stay. Our current notion of the *one* passion week as the duration of Jesus' residence there is then likewise a redactional pattern of Mark's (Luke has not taken it over). Actually the saying cannot altogether be given full value because it is not a

47. E. Lohmeyer, *Galiläa und Jerusalem*, FRLANT NF 34 (1936).

historical saying of Jesus. The speaker originally was a suprahistorical subject, Wisdom.

Time and time again there has been an attempt to find an astronomical point of reference. There are two places especially to which appeal is made: the legend of the star of the Magi (Matt. 2:1 ff.) and the passion narrative. The star of the Magi is said to be an allusion to the conjunction of Jupiter and Saturn in the constellation Pisces in 7 B. C. But one thereby arbitrarily replaces the account of a miraculous moving star with a constellation. Secondly, even so, the year of the birth of Jesus is not thereby ascertained, for the combination of legend and astronomical phenomenon would then simply be explained by saying that people at a later time connected the birth of Jesus with this conjunction of planets. Besides, it is uncertain whether Jesus was born at all during the reign of Herod the Great (thus before 4 B. C.).

We are on better historical ground for the dating of the passion. The tradition (Synoptic and Johannine) is in agreement that Jesus died on a Friday and was raised from the dead on Sunday (Mark 15:42; Matt. 27:62; Luke 23:54; Mark 16:1 par.; John 19:31; 20:1). Of course, according to the Synoptics this Friday was the fifteenth day of the Passover month of Nisan; according to John it was the fourteenth day. Hence in the Synoptics the death of Jesus was on the first day of the feast itself (Mark 14:12 ff.); according to John, it took place on the day before, on the evening of which the Passover lamb was eaten (John 13:1, 29; 18:28; 19:31). It is not possible to harmonize the two datings (not even with the assumption that two different calendars were used). In favor of the Synoptic dating is the general consideration that its presentation stands nearer the facts than the Johannine. Its chronology would be proved accurate if Jesus' last meal really were a Passover meal.[48] But it is first conceived as such in the secondary framework of the account of the institution of the Lord's Supper. One must therefore reckon with the possibility that the death of Jesus was subsequently transferred to the fifteenth of Nisan in order to be able to represent the Last Supper as a Passover. With this position one must also hold that the execution of Jesus took place on the feast day (though one cannot maintain with certainty that such would be impossible; Dalman, J. Jeremias). In general, the Johannine chronology is preferable, especially since it still appears to shine through in Mark 14:1–2 (Dibelius). To be sure, there is a christological motif involved here too: Jesus is executed at the time when the paschal lambs are slaughtered, i.e., he dies as the true paschal lamb (John 19:36; cf. 18:28).

In which year did the fourteenth or fifteenth of Nisan fall on a Friday? Unfortunately the question cannot be answered with certainty since the beginning of the spring month of Nisan was not calculated astronomically, but was ascertained empirically through the observation of the light of the new moon. One possibility is that Friday, 15 Nisan A. D. 30 = April 7, 30 (a weaker possibility: Friday, 14 Nisan, 30). For further possibilities one may consult the tables in Joachim Jeremias's *The Eucharistic Words of Jesus*.[49]

According to Luke 3:23 Jesus was about thirty years old when he made his public appearance. Still, this

48. Eduard Schweizer, "Abendmahl. I. Im Neuen Testament, 6. Jesu letztes Mahl ein Passamahl?" *RGG* 1: 17–18. Eng. trans. by James M. Davis, *The Lord's Supper According to the New Testament*, FBBS 18 (1967), pp. 29–32.

49. Jeremias, *Abendmahlsworte* (cited in the literature for Section 4), p. 16; Eng. trans. by Norman Perrin, *The Eucharistic Words of Jesus* (New York: Scribner's, 3d ed. 1966), p. 38.

assertion is too general and appears too late to be reliable. John 2:20 mentions the forty-sixth year of the construction of Herod's temple, i.e., the year A. D. 27/28.

The net result of all this is that the ministry of Jesus falls in the period around A. D. 30. For the purposes of the historian such a degree of accuracy is exact enough.

5

Birth and Descent

LITERATURE FOR SECTION 5:

Dibelius, Martin. "Jungfrauensohn und Krippenkind: Untersuchungen zur Geburtsgeschichte Jesu im Lukas-Evangelium." Originally in Sitzungsberichte der Heidelberger Akademie der Wissenschaft, Phil.-hist. Klasse Abh. 4, 1932. Reprinted in Dibelius's collected essays, *Botschaft und Geschichte,* vol. 1. Tübingen: Mohr, 1953. Pp. 1–78.

Further literature in Bultmann, *History of the Synoptic Tradition* (cited above, note 10), pp. 291 ff. particularly in the Supplement, pp. 438 ff.

ACCORDING TO the oldest tradition Jesus came from Nazareth in Galilee. To be sure, this name "Nazareth" is not mentioned in Mark 6:1 (where Jesus comes into his *patris,* "his own country"), but this is so only because for Mark the point about Nazareth is self-evident (Mark 1:9, "Jesus came from Nazareth of Galilee"). Mark calls Jesus a "Nazarene" in 1:24; 10:47; 14:67; and 16:6. Bethlehem[50] appears only in the two cycles of legends at the beginning of Matthew and of Luke; it is not the historical place of birth, but one postulated by a definite Christology. The legends through which this is presented can be interpreted meaningfully only under the presupposition of their non-historicity. Both evangelists are in accord in the christological motifs: Jesus is the son of David and the virgin's son. In every detail they disagree. According to Matthew, Joseph and Mary[51] lived first of all in

---

50. E. A. Voretzsch, "Bethlehem," *RGG* 1: 1097–98.
51. Chr. Maurer and E. Hammerschmidt, "Joseph," *RGG* 3: 861 f.; G. Stählin, "Maria," *RGG* 4: 747–48.

Bethlehem. It was only after the birth that they moved—via Egypt—to Nazareth. This is an *ad hoc, artistic* construction. According to Luke, they come—on the basis of the famous census decree—from Nazareth to Bethlehem for the registration. Luke has no accurate idea of the census; this is true as much for the date as for the manner in which it is carried out. The first census in Judea (not Galilee!) took place in A. D. 6/7 (note the date!). This fact is certain on the basis of unequivocal statements in Josephus (*Antiquities* 17. 355 [17. 13. 5]; 18. 1–10 [18. 1. 1]; 20. 102 [20. 5. 2]; *Jewish War* 7. 253 [7. 8. 1]). For only this picture fits the historical situation (take-over of Judea, with direct Roman rule, after the deposition of Archelaus in A. D. 6). The attempts to prove an earlier census (during the time of Herod the Great) are unsuccessful (to agree with Braunert against Instinsky).[52] Such attempts can be supported only from Luke himself and work with a *petitio principii;* they wish to wrest a historical date from a legend which is unsuited for this; for in this way the literary character of these narratives is not taken into consideration. Moreover, Luke himself knows of only *one* census (Acts 5:37), and (against Braunert) he again gives its designation inexactly.

The oldest assertions about Jesus' descent occur in confessional statements which designate him as son of David (Rom. 1:3–4; 2 Tim. 2:8; cf. Mark 10:48; 11:10; 12:35–37). At first this designation was a theologumenon; later there was the attempt to verify it historically by drawing up genealogies (Matt. 1:1 ff.; Luke 3:23 ff.). The non-historicity of these genealogies can be shown by a glance at the Old Testament material used. The two genealogies are not in agree-

---

52. Titles cited in the literature for Section 4.

ment and cannot be brought into congruence. Originally they led to Joseph as the father of Jesus. Later they are combined with the motif of the virginity of Mary (*ante partum*). Neither motif (Jesus as son of David and the virgin's son) reckons with the pre-existence[53] of Christ. Actually the stories of the virgin birth[54] compete with those of the baptism and the transfiguration; they all originally describe a particular time when the divine sonship of Jesus was first established. The notices in Eusebius (*Ecclesiastical History* 3. 20) from Hegesippus concerning the summoning of relatives of Jesus before Domitian cannot prove that the family of Jesus was understood to be Davidic before his public ministry began.

Reliable information about the family of Jesus is meager. We are told the name of his mother, Mary.[55] We hear of brothers and sisters (Mark 6:1–3, cf. Matt. 13:55–56) and are told of Jesus' occupation (or his father's?; the readings diverge): *tektōn*, RSV "carpenter," Mark 6:3. During his lifetime his mother, brothers, and sisters did not belong among his followers (Mark 3:21, 31). After his resurrection Jesus appeared to his brother James[56] (1 Cor. 15:7), who after that time played a prominent role in the Christian community (Gal. 2:9), as do other brothers (1 Cor. 9:5). According to Acts 1:14 Mary also belonged to the community, but without being prominent in it. Paul does not mention her.

Concerning the youth and inner development of Jesus we discover nothing (precisely here there stands at least *one* legend in this gap, that of the twelve-year-old boy, Luke 2:41–52).

53. U. Wilckens, "Präexistenz Christi. I. Im Neuen Testament," *RGG* 5: 491–92.
54. K. Goldammer and W. Marxsen, "Jungfrauengeburt," *RGG* 3: 1068 f.
55. G. Stählin, "Maria," *RGG* 4: 747–48.
56. K. Aland, "Jakobus, Bruder Jesu," *RGG* 3: 525 f.

6

The Locale of the Ministry

LITERATURE FOR SECTION 6:

Lohmeyer, Ernst. *Galiläa und Jerusalem*. FRLANT NF 14 (1937).

Lightfoot, R. H. *Locality and Doctrine in the Gospels*. London: Hodder & Stoughton, 1938.

Conzelmann, Hans. *Die Mitte der Zeit: Studien zur Theologie des Lukas*. Beiträge zur historischen Theologie 17. Tübingen: Mohr, 1954; 2d ed. 1957. Pp. 48 ff. Eng. trans. by Geoffrey Buswell, *The Theology of Luke*. New York: Harper, 1960. Pp. 27 ff.

THE GEOGRAPHICAL FRAMEWORK of the (oldest) gospel, Mark, is a redactional construction which follows the pattern of action in Galilee and passion in Jerusalem (with the journey in Mark 10 as a transition; Lohmeyer).[57] It is self-evident, of course, that historical information stands behind this. Mark has designed the outline here from traditional material, the setting of which was Galilee (Marxsen).[58] Thus Capernaum,[59] above all, is firmly anchored in the tradition. Mark has then worked his material partly into the form of an itinerary. That means that we know the places of Jesus' ministry, but not the movements in particular.

There is therefore no doubt that Jesus first appeared in Galilee. From Galilee was derived the core of his followers (Mark 14:70). This is the case also in John (1:44). The way of Jesus from Galilee to Judea

---

57. *Galiläa und Jerusalem* (cited above, note 47).
58. Willi Marxsen, *Mark the Evangelist: Studies on the Redaction History of the Gospel*, Eng. trans. J. Boyce, D. Juel, W. Poehlmann, with Roy A. Harrisville. New York & Nashville: Abingdon, 1969.
59. K. Galling, "Kapernaum," *RGG* 3: 1133–34.

is also reflected in Matthew and Luke, although here the Markan itinerary has been thoroughly recast. In John a few traditions also point to Samaria (chap. 4). Over against this the long "travel section" or report (Reisebericht) which forms the middle section of Luke has to be located not in Samaria but in Galilee and Judea. In this case one must be aware that the account as a whole is a Lukan construction.

Place is significant in Jesus' ministry in two respects. First, Jesus does not withdraw from the world into the wilderness. Here there is an understanding of his work which clearly contrasts it with that of the Baptist. And secondly he does not turn to the world in general, but to his own people. He does not project a program of world mission, but calls Israel to conversion. With respect to the heathen, Jesus awaits the marvelous gathering of the nations through the direct intervention of God himself (so J. Jeremias[60]; cf. Matt. 8:11–12/Luke 13:28–29). He does not advocate a theoretical (!) universalism;[61] the election of Israel is not contested, but presumed (thus the relative truth of the Jewish Christian logion of Matt. 10:5 f.; cf. 15:24). In terms of content, of course, the radicality of his call to repentance also moves toward a conscious universalism. It becomes operative in this direction after Easter. Here lies an important instance of the continuity between Jesus himself and the later Christian community. For the time being, however, with Jesus himself, universalism expresses itself indirectly, as critical removal of Israel's (religious) security. Israel's election does not replace repentance. Repentance is the sole condition of salvation.

60. *Jesus' Promise to the Nations,* trans. S. H. Hooke, SBT 24 (1958).
61. E. Fuchs, "Universalismus und Partikularismus. III. Im Neuen Testament," *RGG* 6: 1162–64.

7

Beginnings

ALL FOUR GOSPELS report that Jesus was baptized by
John the Baptist.[62] The account is, of course, in its
present form, legend. It remains as a historical fact,
however, that Jesus emerged out of the Baptist's
movement; John's proclamation of the kingdom of
God and call to repentance he acknowledged. We
know nothing more exact about the relationship between the two of them. The Synoptics and the Fourth
Gospel contradict each other concerning the time of
the appearance of Jesus in relation to that of the
Baptist. According to John, the work of the two over-
laps chronologically; according to Mark 1:14, Jesus
first begins his public ministry after the imprison-
ment of the Baptist, i.e., he steps into the breach
which occurs. In the mind of Mark, the Baptist is
thereby represented as the "forerunner" in salvation
history. The juxtaposition also has symbolic meaning
in John's Gospel; in it there is represented the precept
formulated in John 3:30, where the Baptist says of
Jesus, "He must increase, I must decrease."

Throughout the Christian tradition the Baptist is
interpreted as forerunner, but nowhere does he appear as a follower of Jesus. His attitude to Jesus is
reflected in Matthew 11:2 ff./Luke 7:18 ff. Of course,
this material is a creation of the early church which
is intended to represent Jesus as the Promised One.
We do not then know whether or how the Baptist
expressed himself about Jesus. On the other hand,

62. P. Vielhauer, "Johannes, der Täufer," *RGG* 3: 804–808.

Jesus must have taken a positive stand concerning the Baptist. Nowhere is the Baptist opposed. Polemic occurs only against those disciples of the Baptist who preached that the Baptist was himself the messiah and thus came into competition with Christianity (John 1:8, 19 ff.). Jesus' attitude is already expressed in the fact that he—in complete independence—continues the Baptist's eschatology and preaching of repentance. At the same time Jesus' radical new approach is immediately evident when he returned from the wilderness to the inhabited regions, when he did not take over John's ascetic habits (Matt. 11:19/Luke 7:34), and did not baptize (in spite of John 5:22; cf. 4:1). He does not call men away to himself, but rather he seeks them out as the physician who knows himself called to the sick. To this new style of his also belongs the help provided by performing miracles[63] (no miracles are reported of the Baptist). Teaching and conduct, word and deed, proclamation and the anticipatory realization of salvation form a unity. How this self-understanding developed in Jesus psychologically (perhaps as he discovered his miraculous power) is still at most a matter of conjecture. For Jesus did not speak about it; he put into practice that to which he knew himself to be called.

63. G. Mensching et al., "Wunder," *RGG* 6: 1831–37, especially cols. 1834 (in Judaism, by E. Lohse) and 1835 (in the New Testament, by Ernst Käsemann).

8

The Circle of Disciples

LITERATURE FOR SECTION 8:

K. H. Rengsdorf, *"dōdeka"* ("twelve"), in *Theologisches Wörterbuch zum Neuen Testament,* ed. G. Kittel and G. Friedrich, vol. 2. Stuttgart: Kohlhammer, 1935. Pp. 321–28. Eng. trans. by G. W. Bromiley, *Theological Dictionary of the New Testament,* vol. 2. Grand Rapids: Eerdmans, 1964. Pp. 321–28.

——, *"mathētēs"* ("disciple"), ibid., vol. 4 (1942). Pp. 417–64. Eng. trans., 4 (1967). Pp. 415–60.

Schweizer, Eduard. *Erniedrigung und Erhöhung bei Jesus und seinen Nachfolgern.* ATANT 28 (1955). Eng. trans., *Lordship and Discipleship.* SBT 28 (1960).

IT IS SELF-EVIDENT that Jesus gathered around himself a circle of adherents of his own. In the early bits of tradition he appears surrounded by these (Mark 9:14 ff.; 10:13 f., etc.). Individuals are accentuated (Peter;[64] the sons of Zebedee, e.g., Mark 10:35 ff.), yet without becoming full-bodied personalities. The later tradition has stereotyped the picture so that Jesus now appears constantly surrounded by this circle, while in the old pieces of traditional material he appeared primarily alone (cf. the tension between the framework and the older tradition in such places as Mark 1:21, etc.).[65]

"The twelve" is singled out as a group closer to Jesus, and later the title of "apostle"[66] was conferred

---

64. Erich Dinkler, "Petrus, Apostel," *RGG* 5: 247–49.
65. Bultmann, *History of the Synoptic Tradition* (cited above, note 10), p. 343 f.
66. H. Riesenfeld, "Apostel," *RGG* 1: 497–99.

upon "the twelve." Already for Paul "the twelve" is a fixed concept (1 Cor. 15:5). The constituting of this circle is narrated in Mark 3:13–19; yet this report is nothing more than a catalog of apostles which has been superficially brought into narrative form. There is no specific activity by this circle. Of course, there is the report of a "sending forth" (Mark 6:6 ff.), but concrete tasks, experiences, and results cannot be pointed out. The twelve operate largely as "supers" or actors in a play with walk-on roles. Hence, there is doubt whether this group existed as a closed circle already in the lifetime of Jesus and was not rather first called together through an appearance of the Risen One (1 Cor. 15:5),[67] especially since their relationship to the "disciples" in the broader sense is not clear (Mark 3:14; 4:10–12; cf. Bultmann).[68]

The case for the existence of the group prior to Easter points to the fact that the figure of the betrayer, Judas,[69] as a member of this group would not have been invented. Further, it is claimed, formation of the group corresponds to the eschatology of Jesus: it constitutes anticipatory representation of the eschatological people of the twelve tribes of Israel (Matt. 19:28; Luke 22:30—a saying the genuineness of which is disputed). Hence the conclusion is drawn: this purely eschatological conception of the people of God is in clear contrast with the later idea held by the early Christian community of a "church" and must, therefore, be attributed to Jesus himself (so Kümmel).[70]

67. So P. Vielhauer, "Gottesreich und Menschensohn . . ." (cited in the literature for Section 9), pp. 62–64 (in the reprint, pp. 68–71). Cf. Goguel, *Jesus* (cited under "General Presentations," literature for Section 1), pp. 337–41.
68. *History of the Synoptic Tradition* (cited above, note 10), pp. 343 f.
69. E. Fascher, "Judas Iskarioth," *RGG* 3: 965–66.
70. W. G. Kümmel, *Promise and Fulfillment: The Eschatological Message of Jesus*, trans. Dorothea M. Barton, SBT 23 (1957). See also the other titles cited in the literature for Section 9.

However, at Matthew 19:28/Luke 22:30 the twelve do not represent the nucleus of a people of God to be organized on earth, but are appointed heavenly "judges" for the future.

One way or another, the fact stands that Jesus laid down no regulated life style for his disciples which would distinguish them from the public. Time and time again he calls people into discipleship[71] (Mark 10:17 ff.; Luke 9:57 ff.), and this discipleship is demanded unconditionally. But Jesus does not make this discipleship in the external sense a general condition for salvation, i.e., he establishes no sect. Further, the tradition has preserved no trace of esoteric community meals. The one exception, the Last Supper, confirms the rule. The miraculous feeding, in which scholars often wish to find such a trace, is quite public.

In the relationship of Jesus to his disciples what is specific in his self-understanding is documented: he does not wish to train them—like the rabbis—for later "disciples" in the sense that they take the place of the master as teachers. The form of the present discipleship (Nachfolge) is the only one; the distance between master and disciple remains. It is futile to ask how Jesus might have conceived of the relationship in a long-range view. And he did not look forward to a time of discipleship (Jüngerschaft) after his death (against Kümmel); rather he looked to the imminent kingdom.

71. E. Lohse, "Nachfolge Christi. I. Im NT," *RGG* 4: 1286–88.

9

Jesus' Self-Consciousness
(Christological Titles)

LITERATURE FOR SECTIONS 9 and 10 (The Content of
Jesus' Teaching) :

See, in addition to the various theologies of the New
Testament:

Wrede, William, *Das Messiasgeheimnis in den Evan-
gelien: Zugleich ein Beitrag zur Verständnis des
Markusevangeliums.* Göttingen: Vandenhoeck &
Ruprecht, 1901; 3d ed. 1963. Eng. trans. by J. C. G.
Greig, *The Messianic Secret.* The Library of Theolog-
ical Translations, ed. William Barclay. Cambridge &
London: James Clarke & Co., 1971.

Windisch, Hans. *Der Sinn der Bergpredigt.* Leipzig: J. C.
Hinrichs, 1929, ²1937. Eng. trans. by S. MacLean
Gilmour, *The Meaning of the Sermon on the Mount:
A Contribution to the Historical Understanding of the
Gospels and to the Problem of Their True Exegesis.*
Philadelphia: Westminster, 1951.

Dodd, C. H. "Jesus as Teacher and Prophet." *Mysterium
Christi.* Ed. G. K. A. Bell and A. Deissmann. London:
Longmans, Green, 1930. Pp. 53–66.

Montefiore, C. J. B. *Rabbinic Literature and Gospel
Teachings.* London: Macmillan, 1930.

Wendland, H.-D. *Die Eschatologie des Reich Gottes bei
Jesus: Eine Studie über den Zusammenhang von
Eschatologie, Ethik und Kirchenproblem.* Gütersloh:
Bertelsmann, 1931.

Branscomb, Harvie. *The Teachings of Jesus.* Nashville:
Cokesbury, 1931; 2d ed. 1957.

Linton, Olof. *Das Problem der Urkirche in den neueren
Forschung: Eine kritische Darstellung.* Uppsala:
Lundequist, 1932.

Hoffmann, Richard Adolf. *Das Gottesbild Jesu.* Hamburg: P. Hartung, 1934.

Kümmel, W. G. "Jesus und der jüdische Traditions-gedanke." *ZNW* 33 (1934): 105–130. Reprinted in Kümmel's collected essays, *Heilsgeschehen und Geschichte*, ed. E. Grässer, O. Merk, and A. Fritz, Marburger Theologische Studien 3 (Marburg: Elwert, 1965). Pp. 15–35.

———. *Kirchenbegriff und Geschichtsbewusstsein in der Urgemeinde und bei Jesus.* Symbolae Biblicae Upsaliense 1. Zurich: Max Niehans; Uppsala: Seminarium Neotestamenticum Upsaliense, 1943.

———. "Die Gottesverkündigung Jesu und der Gottesgedanke des Spätjudentums." *Judaica* 1 (1954): 40–68. Reprinted in *Heilsgeschehen und Geschichte* (cited above), pp. 107–25.

———. *Verheissung und Erfüllung.* ATANT 6 (1945, ³1956). Eng. trans. by Dorothea M. Barton, *Promise and Fulfillment: The Eschatological Message of Jesus.* SBT 23 (1957).

———. "Jesus und die Anfänge der Kirche." *Studia Theologica* 7 (1953): 1–27. Reprinted in *Heilsgeschehen und Geschichte* (cited above), pp. 289–309.

———. "Futuristische und präsentische Eschatologie im ältesten Urchristentum." *New Testament Studies* 5 (1958–59): 113–26. Reprinted in *Heilsgeschehen und Geschichte* (cited above), pp. 351–63. Eng. trans., "Futuristic and Realized Eschatology in the Earliest Stages of Christianity," *Journal of Religion* 43 (1963): 303–14.

Taylor, Vincent. *Jesus and His Sacrifice: A Study of the Passion-Sayings in the Gospels.* London: Macmillan, 1937.

———. *The Names of Jesus.* New York: St. Martin's Press, 1953.

———. *The Person of Christ in the New Testament Teaching.* New York: St. Martin's Press, 1958.

Major, H. D. A., T. W. Manson, and C. J. Wright. *The Mission and Message of Jesus.* New York: E. P. Dutton, 1938.

Wilder, Amos N. *Eschatology and Ethics in the Teaching of Jesus.* New York: Harper, 1939; 2d ed. 1950.

Ebeling, H. J. *Das Messiasgeheimnis und die Botschaft des Markusevangelisten.* BZNW 19 (1939).

Cadoux, A. T. *The Theology of Jesus.* London: Nicholson and Watson, 1940.

Meyer, R. *Der Prophet aus Galiläa*. Leipzig: Lunkenbein, 1940.

Grant, F. C. *The Gospel of the Kingdom*. New York: Macmillan, 1940.

———. "Ethics and Eschatology in the Teaching of Jesus." *Journal of Religion* 22 (1942): 359–70.

Bultmann, Rudolf. "Die Frage nach der Echtheit von Mt 16, 17–19." *Theologische Blätter* 20 (1941): 265–79.

Knox, John. *The Man Christ Jesus*. New York and Chicago: Willett, Clark, 1941.

———. *Christ the Lord: The Meaning of Jesus in the Early Church*. New York and Chicago: Willett, Clark, 1945.

Michaelis, W. *Der Herr verzieht nicht die Verheissung*. Bern: Buchhandlung der Evangelischen Gesellschaft, 1942.

Davies, P. E., Jr. "Jesus and the Role of Prophet." *JBL* 64 (1945): 241–54.

Lohmeyer, Ernst. *Gottesknecht und Davidssohn*. Göttingen: Vandenhoeck & Ruprecht, 1945; 2d ed. 1953.

Colwell, E. C. *An Approach to the Teaching of Jesus*. New York: Abingdon-Cokesbury, 1946.

Bornkamm, Günther. "Der Lohngedanke im Neuen Testament." *Evangelische Theologie* 6 (1946–47): 143–66. Reprinted in Bornkamm's collected essays, vol. 2, *Studien zu Antike und Urchristentum*, Beiträge zur evangelischen Theologie 28. Munich: Chr. Kaiser, 1959; 2d ed. 1963. Pp. 69–92. Eng. summary in Bornkamm's *Jesus of Nazareth* (cited above, under "General Presentations," literature for Section 1), pp. 137–43.

McCown, C. C., Jr. "Jesus, Son of Man." *Journal of Religion* 28 (1948): 1–12.

Young, F. W. "Jesus the Prophet." *JBL* 68 (1949): 285–99.

Reicke, Bo. "The New Testament Concept of Reward." In *Aux sources de la tradition chrétienne: Mélanges offerts à M. Maurice Goguel*. Paris & Neuchatel: Delachaux & Niestlé, 1950. Pp. 195–206.

Bieneck, J. *Sohn Gottes als Christusbezeichnung der Synoptiker*. ATANT 21 (1951).

Manson, T. W. *The Servant-Messiah: A Study of the Public Ministry of Jesus*. New York: Cambridge University Press, 1953.

―――. *Jesus and the Non-Jews*. London: Athlone Press, 1955. Reprinted as *Only to the House of Israel? Jesus and the Non-Jews,* FBBS 9 (1964).

―――. "Realized Eschatology and the Messianic Secret." In *Studies in the Gospels: Essays in Memory of R. H. Lightfoot,* ed. D. E. Nineham. Oxford: Blackwell, 1955. Pp. 209–22.

von Campenhausen, Hans. *Kirchliches Amt und geistliche Vollmacht*. Beiträge zur historichen Theologie 14. Tübingen: Mohr, 1953. Pp. 1 ff. Eng. trans. by J. A. Baker, *Ecclesiastical Authority and Spiritual Power in the Church of the First Centuries*. Stanford, Calif.: Stanford University Press, 1969.

Percy, E. *Die Botschaft Jesu: Eine traditionskritische und exegetische Untersuchung*. Lunds universitets årsskrift, NF Series 1, Vol. 49, No. 5. Lund: Gleerups, 1953.

Haas, J. *Die Stellung Jesu zu Sünde und Sünder nach den vier Evangelien*. Freiburg (Schweiz): Universitätsverlag, 1953.

Riesenfeld, H. "Jesus als Prophet." In *Spiritus et Veritas,* festschrift for Karl Kundzins. Ed. Auseklis Societas Theologorum Universitatis Latviensis (in exile). Eutin, Germany: A. Ozolins Buchdruckerei, 1953. Pp. 135–48.

Stählin, G. "Die Gleichnishandlungen Jesu." *Kosmos und Ekklesia,* festschrift for W. Stählin. Kassel: J. Stauda Verlag, 1953. Pp. 1–12.

Fascher, E. "Jesus der Lehrer." *ThL* 79 (1954): 325–42.

Fuchs, Ernst. "Bemerkungen zur Gleichnisauslegung." Ibid., cols. 345–48.

Leivestad, Ragnar. *Christ the Conqueror: Ideas of Conquest and Victory in the New Testament*. London: SPCK, 1954.

Pesch, Wilhelm, CSSR. *Der Lohngedanke in der Lehre Jesu: Vergleichen mit der religiösen Lohnlehre des Spätjudentums*. Münchener Theologische Studien I. Historische Abteilung, vol. 7. Munich: Karl Zink Verlag, 1955.

Kuss, Otto. "Bemerkungen zum Fragenkreis: Jesus und die Kirche im Neuen Testament." *Theologische Quartelschrift* 135 (1955): 28–55, 150–83.

Sjöberg, E. *Der verborgene Menschensohn in den Evangelien*. Lund: Gleerups, 1955.

Burrows, Millar. "Thy Kingdom Come." *JBL* 74 (1955): 1–8.

Roberts, Harold. *Jesus and the Kingdom of God.* London: Epworth Press, 1955.

Daube, David. *The New Testament and Rabbinic Judaism.* London: Athlone Press, 1956.

Jeremias, Joachim. *Jesu Verheissung an die Völker.* Stuttgart: Kohlhammer, 1956. Eng. trans. by S. H. Hooke, *Jesus' Promise to the Nations.* SBT 24 (1958).

Vielhauer, Philipp. "Gottesreich und Menschensohn in der Verkündigung Jesu." In *Festschrift für Günther Dehn,* ed. W. Schneemelcher. Neukirchen: Verlag der Buchhandlung des Erziehungsvereins Neukirchen, 1957. Pp. 51–79. Reprinted in Vielhauer's *Aufsätze zum Neuen Testament.* Theologische Bücherei, 31. Munich: Chr. Kaiser, 1956. Pp. 55–91.

Cullmann, Oscar. *Die Christologie des Neuen Testaments.* Tübingen: Mohr, 1957; 2d ed. 1958. Eng. trans. by S. C. Guthrie and C. A. M. Hall, *The Christology of the New Testament.* Philadelphia: Westminster, 1959; 2d rev. ed. 1963.

Braun, Herbert. *Spätjudisch-häretischer und frühchristlicher Radikalismus.* 2 vols. Beiträge zur historischen Theologie 24. Tübingen: Mohr, 1957.

Vögtle, Anton. "Messiasbekenntnis und Petrusverheissung." *Biblische Zeitschrift* NF 1 (1957): 252–72; 2 (1958): 85–113.

Betz, Otto. "Felsenmann und Felsengemeinde." *ZNW* 48 (1957): 49–77.

Grässer, E. *Das Problem der Parusieverzögerung in den synoptischen Evangelien und in der Apostelgeschichte.* BZNW 48 (1957).

Conzelmann, Hans. "Gegenwart und Zukunft in der synoptischen Tradition." *ZThK* 54 (1957): 277–96. Eng. trans. by Jack Wilson, "Present and Future in the Synoptic Tradition," in *God and Christ: Existence and Province,* by Herbert Braun et al., Journal for Theology and the Church 5. Tübingen: Mohr; New York: Harper & Row, 1968. Pp. 26–44.

Gils, F. "Jésus prophète d'après les Évangiles synoptiques." *Orientalia et Biblica Lovaniensia* 2. Louvain, 1957.

40

Stendahl, Krister, ed. *The Scrolls and the New Testament.* New York: Harper, 1957.

Schubert, Kurt. *Die Gemeinde vom Toten Meer: Ihre Entstehung und ihre Lehren.* Basel: Reinhardt, 1958. Pp. 106 ff. Eng. trans. by John W. Doberstein, *The Dead Sea Community: Its Origin and Teachings.* New York: Harper, 1959.

Schweizer, Eduard. "Der Menschensohn." *ZNW* 50 (1959): 185–209. "The Son of Man." *JBL* 70 (1960): 119–29. "The Son of Man Again." *New Testament Studies* 9 (1962–63): 256–61. The first and third items mentioned are reprinted in Schweizer's collected essays, *Neotestamentica.* Zurich: Zwingli-Verlag, 1963. Pp. 56–84 and 85–92.

THE QUESTION of Jesus' self-consciousness is usually formulated as the question of his "messianic consciousness." It must, however, be conceived more broadly and not exhaust itself with the problem of whether and how Jesus applied the Jewish christological titles to himself. At the same time the use of these titles in the Synoptic tradition forms the point of departure for the inquiry. Analysis can indeed uncover literary strata, but within the oldest strata it is no longer possible to establish a temporal sequence (with the exception, naturally, of the fact that the passion forms the conclusion), and consequently we can no longer recognize anything of a gradual development (see above, Section 2).

a) *Christ (Messiah).* The title of "Christ" is seldom used. It is lacking in the Q source. In most places it is easily recognized as redactional (cf., e.g., Matt. 16:20 with Mark 8:30). Mark 9:41; 13:21; 15:32 are also secondary. There remain three passages the genuineness of which comes into question.

First of all, there is the scene of Peter's confession (Mark 8:27 ff. par.). In older research this has been regarded as the turning point in the ministry of Jesus:

41

the confession of the disciples (through Peter) produces in Jesus the resolution to go to Jerusalem. But the scene owes its place in the gospel as a whole to the compositional work of Mark. Thus no historical deductions can be drawn from it. It also contains no concrete historical material, but is a pictorial narrative representation of the post-Easter faith of the church.

Secondly, in Mark 12:35–37 the question of the relationship of the messiah[72] to David is raised. This obscure passage is often interpreted to mean that Jesus here denies that he is descended from David, but that he maintains his messiahship. Rather it concerns the result of discussions of the Christian community, such as is noticeable also in Acts, which relate to the theologumenon of the son of David. It has to be clarified, in the form of a catechetical question, that the messiah, a descendent of David, is now nevertheless—on the basis of his exaltation—greater than David, that is to say, he is David's Lord. It is the Christology of the formula cited by Paul in Romans 1:3–4.

Finally, the title emerges in the passion, in the trial of Jesus before the Sanhedrin (Mark 14:61). This account is not authentic. It has been formed in the church and ought to be recognized as the point of view under which the church sees the entire passion, specifically the christological point of view (cf. the analyses of Dibelius and Bultmann).[73] To be sure, the fact that Jesus went to Jerusalem seems to prove that he appears as a messianic pretender. Actually it proves only that he wished to call the people as such—together with its leadership—inescapably to repentance.

72. M. Weise, R. Meyer, G. Klein, "Messias," *RGG* 4: 902–907.
73. Martin Dibelius, *From Tradition to Gospel* (cited above, note 10), pp. 178 ff., especially 192–93. R. Bultmann, *History of the Synoptic Tradition* (cited above, note 10), pp. 269–71.

A specific "messianic" consciousness cannot be inferred without further ado.

b) *Son of Man.* The matters relating to the title "Son of man" are more difficult. The concept is found in Mark and Q (also in the special material peculiar to Matthew and to Luke; yet here one cannot methodologically decide with certainty whether the title comes from Q or has been introduced by the evangelists themselves; in many places the latter is clearly the case). Outside the gospels the title is almost completely lacking. Within the gospels it occurs only in the sayings of Jesus. This appears to be a strong argument for its authenticity, especially since in contemporary Judaism[74] the title is confined to limited circles and does not show the vigorous development of titles in Synoptic (and Johannine) usage. Hence research overwhelmingly assumes that Jesus took up this title as a designation of what he was and recoined it.

The Son-of-man sayings transmitted to us fall into three groups, which originally stood side by side without, it is noteworthy, any connections among them. They were partly combined for the first time at the stage of redaction, but without any clear overall conception being attained. There are sayings (a) about the Son of man's present activity (the fact that he has come) on earth (Mark 2:10, 28, etc.; Q: Matt. 8:20/ Luke 9:58); (b) sayings about his coming suffering (these are lacking in Q; Mark 8:31; 9:31; 10:33; 9:2, etc.); and (c) sayings about his parousia upon the clouds of heaven (Mark 8:38; 13:26; 14:62; Q: Matt. 24:27, 37/Luke 17:24, 26; M: Matt. 10:23; L: Luke 17:22).

The second group (b) is to be regarded as *vaticinia ex eventu.* One cannot defend their authenticity by suggesting that Jesus must have foreseen a coming

74. H.-F. Weiss, "Menschensohn," *RGG* 4: 874–76.

life-and-death conflict. For these sayings do not articulate a penetrating analysis of the situation, but a divine necessity for his suffering. This means that this group of sayings comprehend the meaning of the passion from this side of Easter. The first group (a) is often explained as originating through a linguistic misunderstanding: originally (in their Aramaic form), it is said, they did not have to do with "*the* Son of man," but with men in general (Mark 2:28; Matt. 8:20). Over against this interpretation one must insist that here, too, "Son of man" was intended from the beginning as a title and that it is a matter of community formation because these sayings look back at the work of Jesus as something exclusive. Finally (c), the sayings about the *One who is to come* are obviously developed from Daniel 7:13 and are (in the crystallization of the mode of expression involved from "a" human-like figure to "the" Son of man) not conceivable apart from the Christian (community-) exegesis of Daniel 7 and application to the person of Jesus. In actuality here also Jesus' exaltation is already presumed. It should be observed that the Synoptic tradition (as distinguished from Jewish apocalyptic[75]) knows of no other heavenly pre-existence of the Son of man than the time between his exaltation and the parousia.

One other interpretation of the third group of sayings is possible, namely, that Jesus always spoke of the One who is to come as a person other than himself. On this view, the sayings are genuine, but Jesus expects some one else as the Son of man (Bultmann)[76];

---

75. H. Ringgren, "Apokalyptik. II. Jüdische," *RGG* 1: 464–66.
76. *Jesus and the Word* (cited above, under "General Presentations," literature for Section 1), pp. 30–31, 38; and Bultmann's *Theology of the New Testament*, 2 vols., trans. K. Grobel (New York: Scribner's, 1951–55), vol. 1, pp. 29–31. [For this position, see further H. E. Tödt, *The Son of Man in the Synoptic Tradition*, trans. Dorothea M. Barton (Philadelphia: Westminster, 1965).]

it was the church which first identified Jesus with the Son of man. However, this view is contradicted by the *a priori* "Christian" character of the application of the basic Daniel passage. Decisive, then, is the fact that in the oldest stratum of tradition expectation of the kingdom of God is nowhere connected with the Son of man (so Vielhauer; against Rudolf Otto, who sees precisely in the synthesis of these two ideas the specific service which apocalyptic had already performed).[77] This finding is even more striking since in Daniel, in fact, both concepts appear.

If the entire Son-of-man concept is posited as theology of the early church (Gemeindetheologie), one still must explain the fact that the title occurs only on the lips of Jesus. Yet it is possible to do this. The negative finding, namely that this title is never used as an address to Jesus, corresponds to the negative finding with the early christological formulas. Unlike "Christ" and "Son of God," "Son of man" is not a confessional title. Jesus was not *called upon* as Son of man, but *awaited* as such. The juxtaposition of the groups of sayings reflects the three aspects of the early church's faith, which also found expression elsewhere: the church looks back upon the earthly existence of Jesus (group a); it acknowledges in the kerygma its faith in his resurrection (with which an interpretation of the passion is connected) (group b); and it looks forward to the parousia[78] (group c). The synthesis came then in the existence of the church as such. It was only relatively late that the church also consciously produced a synthesis by combining the individual groups of sayings into a whole. The history of

77. P. Vielhauer, "Gottesreich und Menschensohn . . ." (cited above, in the literature for Section 9). R. Otto, *The Kingdom of God and the Son of Man* (cited above, under "General Presentations," literature for Section 1).
78. H. Conzelmann, "Parusie," *RGG* 5: 130–32.

the Synoptic tradition still permits a glance into the individual stages in this process.

One can also corroborate this conclusion—independent of analysis of the Son-of-man passages—from the expectation of the kingdom of God. This expectation is so firmly connected by Jesus with his present ministry that there is no room for another interim figure between the present time and the in-breaking of the kingdom, but neither is there time for his own preceding removal and "parousia." And Jesus does not represent his own relationship to the coming of the kingdom *directly,* as he himself shows with the messianic titles. Rather he does so in the indirectness which characterizes his entire ministry—hence through his preaching and his miracles, through his call to repentance, his interpretation of the command of God, through the disclosure of God's immediacy (Unmittelbarkeit) for sinners and the poor. His "Christology" then is an indirect one.

c) *Servant of God.* As for the title "Servant of God," it is merely necessary to observe that it is entirely lacking in the oldest strata. Once it is taken up—in the latest stratum—it does not characterize Jesus as the suffering one, but as the "savior (Matt. 12:18 ff.). It is particularly striking that the later stratum of the Synoptic tradition occasionally, even though sparingly, works with Isaiah 53, but even then not with the Servant-of-God title. In Matthew 8:17, even Isaiah 53:4 ("he took our infirmities . . .") is cited without any allusion to the Servant of God and the passion. For the assumption that Jesus understood himself as the Servant of God in the sense of Deutero-Isaiah,[79] there is no support at all in the sources.

d) *Son of God.* The title "Son of God"[80] does not

79. H. H. Rowley, "Knecht Jahwes," *RGG* 3: 1680–83.
80. J. Schreiber, "Sohn Gottes. II. Im NT," *RGG* 6: 119–20.

belong to the current Jewish designations of the messiah (if it was used at all as such). All of the passages in the Synoptics which use it fall under the suspicion of being formulations of the church. This is true of the cries of the demons (Mark 3:11, etc.), the parable of the Wicked Vinedresser (Mark 12:6; interpreted with Kümmel),[81] the trial (Mark 14:61; see above, Section 9b), and the "epiphanies" (baptism, temptation, transfiguration). In the epiphany stories the Son-of-God concept is understood "adoptionistically": Jesus *becomes* the Son through the present declaration from heaven; the notion of preexistence[82] is unknown here. The saying about the revealer at Matthew 11:25–27/Luke 10:21 f. is a special case. Here, indeed, sonship is to be understood in the sense of preexistence and, to be sure, in the Hellenistic manner, as the mutual relationship of "knowledge" between father and son.

Of course, one must extend the formulation of the question: Is there shown, in manner and mode, as Jesus speaks of God as his Father, consciousness of his being the Son in a unique way? That Jesus characterizes God as Father[83] is not surprising in Judaism. The question, however, is whether he spoke in an exclusive sense of "his" Father. According to the Synoptics he did. For he speaks, on the one hand, of "my" Father (Matt. 7:21) and, on the other hand, of "your" Father (Matt. 5:45), but he never embraces both himself and his hearers with the phrase "our" Father. But this consistent distinction proves to be the style of the church's tradition (Gemeindetradition),

81. W. G. Kümmel, *Promise and Fulfillment* (cited above, note 70), pp. 40, 82 f.
82. U. Wilckens, "Präexistenz Christi," *RGG* 5: 491–92.
83. E. Fascher, "Gott. IV. Im NT, 2. Jesu Gott-Vater-Glaube," *RGG* 2: 1715–16. J. Jeremias, "Vatername Gottes. III. Im NT," ibid. 6: 1234–35.

especially since most passages with the title Father are secondary. Scholars further make appeal to the address *"abba."* This term is said to reflect intimacy and to exhibit a consciousness of the nearness to God unheard of within Judaism. Yet this does not prove to be an *exclusive* word-usage (to agree with Herbert Braun),[84] for *"abba"* was also used as a term of address in the church (Rom. 8:15).

For all this, there is no doubt that Jesus possessed the consciousness of a singular bond with God. But here, too, it must be maintained that this expresses itself (only) indirectly.

e) *The Messianic Secret.* According to Mark, Jesus did not openly designate himself as messiah or Son of God (and when he spoke of the Son of man, it was in a way which would veil his identity). It was first when he stood captive before the Council and was asked whether he was "the messiah, the Son of the Blessed" that he said, "I am he" (*egō eimi,* Mark 14:61–62). During his public ministry he forbade the sick whom he had healed to relate anything about it (Mark 7:36); he forbade the demons to "reveal" that he was the Son of God (Mark 3:11–12). Above all, after Peter's confession and the transfiguration, he demanded from the disciples silence about his nature —until the resurrection.

This secrecy can scarcely be historical fact. In the way in which it is reported it is not at all conceivable and in itself is full of contradictions. The directions for secrecy about a miracle often stand in cross contradiction to the setting. Also, the secrecy motif is not present in the early bits of tradition, but in the redactional framework, in summaries. It is, then, a theory which was only subsequently drawn up. Wrede[85]

---

84. Herbert Braun, *Radikalismus* (cited above, note 39), vol. 2, pp. 127–28, note 2.
85. *Das Messiasgeheimnis in den Evangelien* (cited above, note 8).

wished to explain it in a historical-pragmatic way: the community created it in order to remove the contradiction between the unmessianic character of the tradition and its own messianic faith (see above, Section 1). This explanation is improbable, for the secrecy theory was first produced at a time when there was no longer a *consciousness* of an unmessianic character of the tradition. It served rather for the positive presentation of a doctrine of revelation—conceived in the sense of paradox! It is significant that Mark (who was probably the originator of the theory), in applying it, had to work hardest in those places where the traditional material (already in the pre-Markan stage) was most strongly "messianic," e.g., in connection with the transfiguration (Mark 9:9).

f) *Results.* All of this indicates that Jesus' self-consciousness is not comprehensible in terms of the christological titles. These titles were conferred on him by the faith of the church. Furthermore, on methodological grounds the words in which Jesus speaks of his "being sent" ("I came . . ." Mark 2:17*b*, etc.) must be set aside, for they have been formulated in retrospect, looking back at his completed ministry. In any case, no methodological certainty can be attained here.

We must therefore inquire of the picture of his ministry as a whole, as it confronts us in the oldest stratum of the tradition. Such a picture can in fact be distinguished clearly. We see Jesus as miracle worker and teacher, who understands these two aspects as a unity. For in his eschatological teaching he refers to his deeds as signs of what is coming (Mark 13:28–29), and in his exposition of the commandments he inserts himself as the authoritative interpreter: "But I say to you . . ." In deed and teaching, he confronts the amazed people *directly* with God through himself. In his figure one can find traits of the prophet as well as of the rabbi. For he discloses the future in that he announces the in-breaking of the kingdom of God. He argues in the style of Jewish debates about the torah (cf. the style of the scholastic dialogues and controversy stories [*Schul- und Streitgespräche*]!) and is also addressed as "rabbi" (Mark 9:5, etc.); and he gathers pupils around himself. From him, wisdom sayings are transmitted. Even if their genuineness is questionable in individual cases, as an aggregate they nonetheless as a result leave an impression on hearers.

The concepts of prophet and rabbi, however, express only a partial aspect and not exactly the core of the matter. Jesus understands himself as the one who makes the *final* appeal. His place is unique, since after him nothing more "comes"—but God himself. So he approaches the public and reveals what is coming. He does this not in the form of a *picture* of the future, but in such a way that while futurity is retained as such, at the same time it becomes effective in the present encounter (or: *as* encounter), as healing of the sick, blessing of the poor. He teaches about the will of God in such a way that at the same time he opens up the realization and makes intelligible the unity of command and freedom, first in his own conduct: in breaking through the cultic legislation (sabbath regulations, Mark 2:23 ff.; 3:1 ff.; prescriptions about clean[86] and unclean, Mark 7:1–23), in the sovereignty of proclaiming salvation to sinners, publicans, and prostitutes, and judgment to the self-assured.

86. E. Lohse, "Rein und Unrein. III. Im NT," *RGG* 5: 944.

10

The Content of Jesus' Teaching

LITERATURE FOR SECTION 10: See Section 9, above.

JESUS DID NOT draw up any system of teaching. It strikes one, on the contrary, that at first glance his teaching about God and his eschatology, his eschatology and ethics appear to stand alongside one another in a relatively disconnected way. But his statements do exhibit a perfect consistency if one carries through a complete assessment. The primary element is the absoluteness of the promise of salvation (Heilszusage). It takes shape in the presentation of God as Father, i.e., in the recovery of immediacy to him through the proclamation of forgiveness. Precisely from this follows the radical understanding of the demand of God which—in its unconditional nature—carries with it its fulfillment, and the understanding of the present time as the last hour, which opens up access to the kingdom of God.

Salvation in its unconditional nature is the crisis of all security (*securitas*). The message detaches the individual from the group which provides security (Israel) and opens him to his neighbor by making love possible. Jesus' attitude is thereby set toward Israel and toward the elements of its existence (election, scripture, law, tradition), just as is his attitude to individuals (as sinner or righteous person, poor or rich). The connection of salvation with the person of Jesus lies simply in the fact that *he* offers this salvation as present, final possibility, that he now comforts the poor, and calls sinners to himself. Indirect Christology and the-ology [i.e., the concept of God] are brought into congruence.

The form of Jesus' teaching corresponds to the content. Jesus does not summon people to an objective consideration of God, the world, and man, but he grasps the hearer directly and reveals his situation through "beatitudes" (*makarismos*), the prophetic call, threats (Drohwort), through illumination in the style of wisdom, through his parables.[87] Even his interpretation of scripture is not that of a detached observer, but is "actualizing" (aktualisierend).[88]

a) *Fundamentals* (*Law, Scripture, Tradition, Israel*). The law[89] is valid; you have it in scripture. It is not expressly substantiated, but is presumed. Jesus proceeds, then, from the common Jewish viewpoint. But immediately, what is new is expressed; it lies in Jesus' concentration on a pointed overall understanding. For Judaism, the interpretation by which one can recognize and fulfill the will of God belongs to the law.[90] This leads either to casuistry[91] or to a heightening of the torah in the sense of the "Rule of the Community" (1QS) at Qumran[92] (Herbert Braun). Over against this interpretation and practice, Jesus places a new and peculiarly dialectical method of exposition. He assumes that the law is intelligible by itself and needs no interpretation at all. Such interpretation is the work of men and obscures the matter; it is a question of getting back behind the human precepts to the

87. N. A. Dahl, "Gleichnis und Parabel. II. 3. Im NT," *RGG* 2: 1617–19.
88. G. Bornkamm, "Formen. II. Im NT, 1. Die Jesus-Überlieferung," *RGG* 2: 999–1002; ibid., "Evangelien, formgeschichtlich," 2: 749–53.
89. O. Bauernfeind, "Gesetz. IV. Im NT, 1. Jesus," *RGG* 2: 1517–18.
90. E. Lohse, "Gesetz. III. Im Judentum," *RGG* 2: 1515–17.
91. E. L. Dietrich, "Kasuistik. II. Jüdische," *RGG* 3: 1167–68.
92. M. Burrows et al., "Qumran," *RGG* 5: 740–56, especially 741. For Braun, "Toraverschärfung," see above, note 39.

commandments themselves. The law is no longer a court of appeal between God and me, nor a means of placing me in a relationship to him. Instead, it is his "instantaneous" word to me, which precisely reveals the immediacy and instantaneously discloses the deed to me. His commandment and his attitude, which is one of goodness that showers us with gifts, form a unity.

This understanding of God and law must lead to a conflict with the entire scribal casuistry in which, according to Jesus, God's will is not explained but distorted (Mark 7:6–7) and to a protest against the division of outer and inner which is unavoidable in legalism. There is no possibility of a neutral position (parable of the Talents Entrusted, Matt. 25:14–30/ Luke 19:11–27). The word of the precept (even that set down in scripture) can be suspended in the specific case for the sake of obedience (e.g., permission for divorce, Mark 10:1 ff. par.). Jewish Christianity[93] later failed to carry through with this freedom (Matt. 5:17–20).

The Jewish practices of piety (fasting, etc., Matt. 6:16 ff.; cf. the entire section!) and of the cult (Matt. 5:23 f.) are not abrogated. Jesus' battle rather was with the hypocrisy[94] which uses them as a means; they cannot protect from God, or take the place of repentance. It is from this perspective that the threats against Jerusalem and the temple are formulated (Mark 13:2–3; Matt. 23:37 ff.; Luke 13:34 f.; the cleansing of the temple, Mark 11:15 ff.). The cult is perverted if one uses it to evade the commandment; the sabbath is abused if one denies love for its sake (Mark 3:1 ff.).

93. W. G. Kümmel, "Judenchristentum. I. Im Altertum," *RGG* 3: 967–72.
94. G. Bornkamm, "Heuchelei," *RGG* 3: 305–306.

Israel is in fact elected; this, indeed, is presumed as self-evident and is not discussed as a problem. But here one notices the reduction: Jesus has no interest at all in a theory of salvation history. He does not trace the ways of God in the history of his people, but points Israel to the present moment as the final one, one in which it lays hold of its election or, on the other hand, finally nullifies it. One cannot claim the state of election objectively; otherwise one discovers, "Many will come from east and west and recline at table with Abraham and Isaac and Jacob in the kingdom of heaven; but the children of the kingdom will be cast out into outer darkness" (Matt. 8:11–12). "Israel" is not salvation and does not guarantee it. Here, too, one discovers the radical separation which leads to a community of a new kind. It is immediately obvious that this preaching had to lead to a fundamental conflict with *all* the trends within Judaism. Only the preaching of the Baptist presents a special case.

b) *Concept of God*. Jesus wished to formulate no new doctrine of God.[95] He believed in the God of Israel, the Creator and Ruler, Lawgiver and Judge. He did not define God's "essence," but brought his lordship to bear in its absoluteness; and this absoluteness is salvation. Naturally, God has "attributes"; he is righteous and good—indeed the only good One (Mark 10:18). This, however, is not an analysis of his "being," but a statement about his relationship to the world. All assertions about God include at once the hearer who is addressed: he is Father. To be sure, this concept does not occur very frequently in the authentic sayings, but it reproduces the structure of the God-relationship adequately.

95. E. Fascher, "Gott. IV. Im NT," *RGG* 2: 1715–17.

The insight that God rules *directly* leads to the overcoming of anxiety (Matt. 6:25 ff.). We find in Jesus the motifs of popular belief in providence (Matt. 10:29 ff.), but no theory concerning providence and God's perpetual activity. Rather we find revealing indications of specific concrete experience of this (e.g., in the observation of happenings in nature), for God allows himself to be known in the world. This view has nothing to do with a systematically designed *theologia naturalis* or with a theoretical proof of God. Jesus has no concept of "nature." His indications are actual address.

Since God's governance is not analyzed from a distance, but is revealed as something which one comes to experience, the relationship of his providence to breakthroughs of the normal world order via miracles[96] poses no intellectual difficulties. Jesus does not reflect at all about the general possibility of miracle. The idea of natural law is foreign to him; thus with him there is no *concept* of miracle. In purview lie only the deeds which he himself does. (Naturally there is not any doubt that God can intervene in his own way at any time; but such reflections do not become the subject of his teaching.) Further, miracle is a way in which God makes himself intelligible, and it happens *hic et nunc*. In this way the very fact that Jesus is present (das Da-Sein Jesu) is drawn into the proclamation about God. Miracle is a present "sign," not an objective proof. Therefore it cannot serve as a theoretical proof about God. Rather the experience of miracle, for its part, presupposes belief in God.[97]

That God does *all,* that he lays claim to *my* conduct

---

96. E. Käsemann, "Wunder. IV. Im NT," *RGG* 6: 1835–37.
97. R. Bultmann, *Jesus and the Word* (cited above, under "General Presentations," literature for Section 1), pp. 172–79.

(and at the same time makes it possible), and that he permits me to ask him to do something special for myself or some other person which he would not do apart from my request, that is the unitary conception of faith which becomes directly intelligible in the situation of prayer.[98] Precisely because God is omnipotent, one can turn to him without fear (Jesus does not know the Jewish fear of pronouncing God's name; in Jewish Christianity one can observe a certain regression on this matter). Because he rules, one can ask with confidence, in the trust that God already knows what we need (Matt. 6:7–8; 7:7 ff.). The one who prays is summoned by God himself to turn to him and ask the impossible. He may hope for fulfillment, but he cannot calculate on this. Prayer has as its norm: "Your will be done," and this will is good for me (Matt. 7:9 ff.). Even Satan[99] does not become a problem of universal (weltanschaulich) proportions. Evil and its origin are not explained. Satan is "the" evil (one), whose power is not balanced against the omnipotence of God, but is bound (Mark 3:23 ff. par.).

In all of this the relationship with God is understood to be established by God unilaterally (and mediated through Jesus). Quantitatively, of course, the concept of faith[100] plays no considerable role, but the phenomenon itself is worked out clearly. Faith is the complete renunciation of calculation, of the interposing of performances as an intermediate court of appeal (Luke 17:1 ff.). It is the "simple" receiving of God's gifts, and its structure corresponds to this. God indeed gives unconditionally. He causes his sun to

98. O. Bauernfeind, "Gebet. IV. Im NT, 3. Jesus," *RGG* 2: 1220–21.
99. F. Horst, "Teufel. II. Im AT, Judentum und NT," *RGG* 6: 705–707.
100. H. Braun, "Glaube. III. Im NT, 2. Jesus von Nazareth," *RGG* 2: 1591–92.

shine and makes it rain on the good and the evil (Matt. 5:45). He is—from the standpoint of performance and calculating "righteousness'—exasperatingly gracious (parable of the Laborers in the Vineyard, Matt. 20:1–15). At this point the message of salvation is brought into conflict with those who advocate man's accomplishments before God.

It is self-evident that the limitlessness of this goodness does not mean that evil is not taken seriously, but is the challenge to give, in the same way (Luke 6:36/Matt. 5:48). Just because God's goodness is offered without condition, one can only receive it ("as a child," Mark 10:15), but not cultivate it for oneself toward God. And one cannot reckon on it in advance. The "prodigal son" (Luke 15:11 ff.) can return home. But he cannot repeat his behavior a second time in the confidence that his father would thus be good in the same way. God's "goodness" is received above all as the forgiveness of sins. I cannot detach the acceptance of this from my own behavior; otherwise I forfeit it (parable of the Unmerciful Servant, Matt. 18:23–35). Consequently the petition for forgiveness is joined to the acknowledgement of my own readiness to forgive (Matt. 6:12/Luke 11:4).

Jesus understands his preaching as an invitation in God's own name. This is substantiated by the manner and method in which he speaks of sin[101] and of man's sinfulness. Here also he joins with Jewish presuppositions. It can simply be taken as a given fact that man is a sinner and commits sins (Matt. 7:11: "You, who are evil"). Mankind is an evil and rebellious generation (Matt. 16:4). Everyone knows what sin is, for he knows the commandments. Not to understand this is obstinacy. Thus there is no theory *about* sin (e.g., in

101. K. Stendahl, "Sünde und Schuld. IV. Im NT," *RGG* 6: 484–89.

the form of a doctrine of original sin). Jesus speaks unreflectively of good and evil, the righteous and unrighteous. This is only apparently contradictory to what has just been established. One can understand it if he conceives of the words of Jesus here also as the immediate conveying of the presence (Da-Sein) of God. The saying about God's goodness toward the good and the evil does not contain an invitation to a neutral contemplation of this goodness. It is aimed at me and seeks to make me good. I cannot use it in order to assert my own goodness—toward God—and to renounce his forgiveness. But just as little can I look at my neighbor there in his sinfulness. If I do that, then I discover: "If you do not repent, you will likewise perish" (Luke 13:3, 5; cf. Matt. 7:2 ff.). Sinfulness is thus not analyzed, but time and again revealed so that it will be experienced *coram Deo* ("before God"), under the aspect of forgiveness. Hence there is a battle against evil, but not the pathos of anger (Matt. 5:39), not even in the conflict sayings against the rich, the righteous, and the secure. There is no doubt that the world is in a bad state, that Satan rules. But even evil is measured from the perspective of God's turning to us. Powerful rulers (Mark 10:42) and mammon (Luke 16:9) reign, but there is no question of setting force against force (Matt. 5:39). Rather it is a question of overcoming evil through good.

Over against a "consistent eschatological" interpretation of the teaching of Jesus it must be emphasized that where God's governance as such is developed, the prospect of the imminent end of the world is lacking. The world appears simply as creation, the sphere of the rule and care of God. One understands the relationship to the eschatological assertions if he pays attention to the *direction* of the thought of Jesus. Jesus repeatedly makes a fresh start, and again and again

with Jewish concepts—in the case of monotheism[102]
and faith in the Creator; again, in connection with
the law, in an equally original way; and, once again,
with regard to eschatology. However, he does not at-
tain a unity in these areas by establishing a logical
connection. On the contrary, it is striking in how few
instances this is the case. On the one hand, Jesus bases
the call to repentance on the nearness of the kingdom
of God, but he establishes the material demand with
a *general* reference to the God who commands. The
question becomes all the more urgent whether a uni-
fied idea of existence can be perceived in his doctrine
of God, ethics, and eschatology. As a matter of fact,
such is the case. The intention everywhere is for a
confrontation of man with God without any inter-
mediary. The shrinking of time in eschatology corresponds to the enlargement of space as the place of
faith and obedience in the doctrine of God and eschatology. The unity of these areas is given in the person
of Jesus, who is the one who makes the disclosure in
both cases. The question of whether salvation is also
possible without him is misleading—in view of the
fact that it is through him the signs occur.

c) *The Will of God (Ethics)*. With regard to the
will of God (ethics) the main problem has already
been pointed out: How are eschatology and ethics
related to one another for Jesus? Is the proclamation
of the kingdom of God the central ethical motive
("Repent, *for* the Kingdom of God has drawn near,"
Mark 1:14 f.), so that Jesus' ethics could be charac-
terized as an "interim ethics,"[103] therefore as instructions limited to the brief, final time span (as Albert
Schweitzer proposed)? If that were the case, Jesus'

102. W. Schmauch, "Monotheismus und Polytheismus. III. Im
Urchristentum," *RGG* 4: 1115–16.
103. H. van Oyen, "Interimsethik," *RGG* 3: 792.

ethics would stand, but would also fall, with the imminent (!) expectation of the end.

The observation is decisive that the nearness of the kingdom indeed motivates the general call to repentance, but that no content of the demand is derived from it; the content derives rather from the will of God revealed in the commandments. Furthermore, even if in fact now is the last hour, God will not will anything today other than what he has always willed.

Thus it is established that eschatology and ethics are not logically subordinated or set one over the other, but that both represent analogous ways of carrying out the direct confrontation. The content of the demand is not just related to the doctrine of God through means of eschatology, but directly—whether it be that one simply cites the Old Testament commandment, or that one emphasizes God's demand for accountability (parable of the Talents Entrusted, Matt. 24:14–30/Luke 19:11–27), or that one points to God's providence which liberates us from anxiety and enables us to practice love. As in the doctrine of God, so also in ethics, Jesus can appeal to rational discernment (Einsicht) (Luke 12:57 ff.); for if God's rule as a whole is intelligible, so also is his will. This is the presupposition for overcoming legalism. And just as in that case, so also here the appeal is not derived as part of a theory (about the natural ability to comprehend a rational moral code). The concept of God is presumed throughout. A rational autonomous foundation for ethics is totally beyond the horizon of Jesus. And faith in God is not simply the (formal) acceptance of the fact that God exists and makes demands, but is the concrete acceptance of salvation. The ethics of Jesus then shows how God's goodness which encounters us is to be transposed into contemporary actualization. Ethics stands under the sign of the gospel which reaches us in Jesus' preaching. His person is included in the interpretation of the commandment: "But *I* say to you." We saw above the dialectic which is contained in this "exposition" ("Auslegung") of scripture: it exists precisely in the indication that the commandment is already interpreted from within itself.

If I understand God—and that I can do—then I understand also the *absoluteness* of his commandment. I understand that he not only wants *something* from me, he wants *me* (G. Bornkamm).[104] The inner —the will—and the outer—the act—cannot be separated. Precisely those sayings which juxtapose the inner and the outer and assign preeminence to the former (Mark 7:6 ff., 17 ff.; Luke 11:34 ff.) aim not at an independent inwardness, but at wholeness. They do not say that the intention is the chief thing and not the action, but that the intention is also an act and that I certainly cannot establish my goodness by carrying out individual good deeds. Rather the quality of my deeds is determined through the whole of my being (cf. the figure of the tree and its fruit, Matt. 7:16 ff.). Thus wholeness stands (as God's gift) at the beginning and not at the end (as a result of my performance; compare over against this the ethics of Aristotelianism and Scholasticism). Jesus knows no abstract concept of the subject, nor does he know the idea of *liberum arbitrium* ("free will"). One can illustrate this by considering the anthropological concept of the heart. I am not first of all "free," judging the claim which is made upon me; in that moment the point of the claim would already be missed. In a single moment it becomes clear and intelligible and immediately lays claim to me. In obeying or refusing to

104. Cf. Bornkamm, *Jesus of Nazareth* (cited above, under "General Presentations," literature for Section 1), pp. 96–152.

obey I do not do something which can be detached from me, the doer, as a "work." In my deed I myself am at stake; I gain or lose myself.

Thus ethics cannot be presented as teaching about virtues. Nor can the problem of autonomy versus heteronomy even arise. Jesus' ethics is heteronomous in so far as a command is set before me from outside; and it is *not* heteronomous in that God commands that through which I gain myself, and in that his command carries with it (in my own deed) its accomplishment. Obedience is not formal; otherwise it would not be complete. Out of the completeness of the demand the individual commandment becomes intelligible to me; I can perceive why God wills precisely this and not something else. I can conceive that the commandments, "You shall not kill, commit adultery, etc.," are intended by God himself as radically as Jesus "expounds" ("auslegt," see two paragraphs above) them in the antitheses of the Sermon on the Mount,[105] so that lust is already adultery. The unfolding of God's will in detail does not lead to a new casuistry because in this the unitary meaning is uncovered, viz., the command of love,[106] which tolerates no limitation—thus it even includes the love of enemies.

The double commandment of love for God and neighbor (Mark 12:28–34) is not new; it is derived from the Old Testament (Deut. 6:4–5; Lev. 19:18). Jesus simply establishes its absoluteness. There is no case in which love would not be commanded. The demand to love your neighbor "as yourself" tolerates no protective restriction (Kierkegaard).[107] The ques-

---

105. G. Bornkamm, "Bergpredigt. I. Biblisch," *RGG* 1: 1047–50, especially col. 1048.
106. N. A. Dahl, "Liebe. III. Im NT," *RGG* 4: 364–67.
107. Cf. Bornkamm, *Jesus of Nazareth* (cited above, under "General Presentations," literature for Section 1), pp. 113 f., quoting

tion of whether the enemy means only my personal enemy or also the enemy of the group or of the nation is as misguided as the other question of who is my "neighbor" (parable of the Good Samaritan, Luke 10:25–37). Love of God and love of neighbor are distinguished and yet are not two different things. Love for the neighbor is not somehow the means of loving God (Bultmann).[108] I should love my neighbor for God's sake, which is to say that now more than ever I should see him as my fellow man (Mitmenschen). He is not degraded into a means through which I practice love for God. Love of neighbor is rather the concretizing of my love to God. Love is not the highest value (virtue) on a scale of values; it can appear as the crisis of all moral values. I do not know beforehand what love is in the particular situation (love, therefore, is no formal principle). In the encounter I cannot first consider love objectively. Nor do I need to do this, because love discloses itself in the moment.

The notion of accomplishment and of the earning of salvation through "good works" is left behind at the outset. There is the further result that the problem of the conflict of obligations cannot arise at all. When it does emerge in the discussion, it is only in order to reject it, to unmask it as being spurious (e.g., in the conflict between cult and love, Matt. 5:23–24; Mark 7:9 ff.). The Jewish formulation of the question in terms of higher and lower commandments is not

Kierkegaard's *Leben und Walten der Liebe,* Ger. trans. by Schrempf (pp. 19–20); Eng. trans. of Kierkegaard by Howard and Edna Hong, *Works of Love: Some Christian Reflections in the Form of Discourses* (London: Collins, 1962), pp. 34–35.
108. R. Bultmann, *Jesus and the Word* (cited above, under "General Presentations," literature for Section 1), pp. 110–120, especially 115.

only answered but is also transcended through reference to the love commandment (Mark 12:28-34).

In the face of this radicality there is the question of the possibility of fulfillment of the commandment.[109] For Jesus this cannot become the principal problem. He takes for granted that the moment I understand the obligation, the ability to do it is also disclosed. The fulfillment too is a gift. The problem of obedience and grace vanishes (H. Braun).[110] One cannot consider, even for a moment, either the commandment as such or the question of its fulfillment apart from God's specific way of acting toward us, apart from the gift of forgiveness.

If love is the fulfillment of obedience, the thought of merit before God cannot arise. Love cannot ask for profit which accrues to me myself; otherwise it annuls itself. An obedience which asks for reward is no obedience. It is a matter of: "When you have done all the things commanded, then say, 'We are unprofitable servants; we have done what we ought'" (Luke 17:10). It is no contradiction if we at the same time assert that not only does a notion of reward exist in the teachings of Jesus, but that it is even a constitutive element, not one to be eliminated. Here, also, interpretation has to keep in mind, as point of departure, the Jewish understanding of the motif and must see the direction in which this understanding has been developed. The notion of reward is not somehow dragged along as excess baggage from the Jewish world—an idea embarrassing for modern sensitivities (such as it appeared by and large where

109. G. Bornkamm, "Bergpredigt. I. Biblisch," *RGG* 1: 1047-50, especially cols. 1049-50; and E. Fascher, "II. Auslegungsgeschichtlich," ibid., 1050-53, especially col. 1053.
110. Braun, *Radikalismus* (cited above, note 39), vol. 2, pp. 132-35.

theology stood under the influence of Kant's ethics[111]). The idea of reward is actually incorporated into the total conception of God and man. In the simplicity of the father-child relationship the aspect of calculation is brushed aside. From this perspective, reward becomes a matter of pure promise. One can receive it "as a child." The notion of reward expresses the fact that the message is about *me,* that it is salvation, that I may hope *for myself.* Whoever loses his life hears the promise that he will gain it (Luke 9:24; 17:33).

Since the will of God is intelligible in the situation, Jesus does not need to strive for completeness. His directions are actually a disclosure (Ent-deckung), an indication of that which is "self-evident"—within the framework of faith. He projects no program for shaping the world. His horizon is Palestinian, Jewish, and rural. For that reason there is no comprehensive discussion laid out in the areas of culture or politics, either in the form of an ordering of values or in the form of a systematic critique. Jesus demands no revision of the law—let alone its repeal—but the individual's renunciation of his practice of using the law for his own advantage. This renunciation is a specific decision, not a new, general world order. And it is not passive submission, but positive confrontation in accordance with the love commandment, made possible through the lack of anxiety which comes from trust in God (Matt. 5:38 ff.). Thus Jesus does not demand that the oath[112] as an institution be abolished, but he forbids swearing (Matt. 5:33 ff., cf. 23:16 ff.), i.e., he commands truthfulness. This makes swearing superfluous. Truthfulness is possible where I am relieved

---

111. D. Henrich, "Kant, Immanuel," *RGG* 3: 1123–27, especially cols. 1125–26.
112. O. Bauernfeind, "Eid. III. Im NT und in der christlichen Kirche, 1," *RGG* 2: 350–51.

of anxiety about myself and mistaken machinations to save myself are no longer necessary. Just as little is the legislation regarding marriage reformed, but divorce is forbidden, in which case the presupposition concerning marriage is disclosed (Mark 10:1 ff. par.). Divorce is forbidden as well as lust (Matt. 5:27 ff.).[113] Matthew 5:32 and 19:9 show how this unconditional demand was later transposed into a practicable legal code (Rechtsordnung) in the church.

In the social sphere Jesus projected no new order of society and property. He demands neither the emancipation of slaves nor the equalization of property. He calls the poor "blessed" in that he reveals their eschatological situation.[114] But he does not include them in the threat against the rich. This threat also is eschatologically determined. Both groups are pointed to God, not to each other. Here, too, there is no mutual watching and judging. Jesus does not call for social revolution, and he nurses no resentment. Property is not forbidden, but Jesus does show its danger for the owner (Mark 10:25). In a particular case he can demand a voluntary, total renunciation of property (Mark 10:17 ff.), but no general rule is derived from this. Renunciation is only then a condition of salvation when Jesus calls into his discipleship— this means that it is a condition as a *decision*, not as a *state*. It is not the riches of the farmer which are criticized, but his folly in relying on these (Luke 12: 13–21). When the kingdom of God comes, the poor will no longer be poor and the rich will no longer be rich. Hence both have the criterion for the present time. Only at the edge of Jesus' thought does the idea of compensatory justice emerge—in the parable of the Rich Man and Lazarus (Luke 16:19–31); yet it is

113. H. Greeven, "Ehe. III A. Im NT, 1. Jesus," *RGG* 2: 318–19.
114. E. Kutsch, "Armut. I. Biblisch, 1," *RGG* 1: 622–23.

conditioned through the prehistory of the parabolic material involved; it is not thematically developed.

Politics is visible only marginally. For Judaism the political dominion of Rome was also a religious problem. God's dominion and the political place of the Jewish people hang together. Jesus, however, separates them completely and brings to bear the purely eschatological character of the kingdom of God. He explains that the place of Rome is not a problem which touches upon faith (cf. the discussion about the tribute money, Mark 12:13–17). One cannot calculate obedience toward Caesar and toward God as being of the same order. The statement that one should give to Caesar what is Caesar's and to God what is God's does not mean a relativizing (so that, as it were, both claims enjoy equal rights). Here Jesus points precisely to the absoluteness of obedience toward God. Because one must obey him unconditionally, he cannot use God's name in order to cover over a worldly political program. One cannot use God as a given entity, nor can one use him for the benefit of the "chosen people."

All these ethical instructions aim not at a retreat from the world, but at the restoration of the freedom of the children of God in his world (although the concept of freedom does not play a part in this). The sayings about anxiety do not forbid daily work,[115] but presuppose it as the normal thing. They project no ideal "romantic-vegetative" life style—for this would still not be the overcoming of anxiety. On the other hand, Jesus does not abolish the Jewish practice of fasting (Matt. 6:16 ff.), but he demands no ascetic practice. He himself indeed did not take over the asceticism[116] of the Baptist and for that reason was reproached as a glutton and a drunkard (Matt. 11:19).

115. W. Bienert, "Arbeit. III. Theologisch," *RGG* 1: 539–45.
116. K. G. Kuhn, "Askese. IV. Im Urchristentum," *RGG* 2: 642–44.

d) *The Announcement of the Kingdom of God.*

i) The Problem. Jesus stands in the tradition of Jewish eschatology.[117] On this basis it is comprehensible that statements about God's rule and statements about the coming of his kingdom stand beside one another in a disconnected way. But here too one can recognize the essential connection by looking back at the starting point. Because God is God, one can point to his universal world rule as well as to his future assuming of dominion, and this assertion by Jesus is itself a factor in the event.

The Jewish substratum is evident in the fact that the concept of the kingdom of God[118] is not explained but presumed to be understood. (Matthew favors the expression, "kingdom of heaven," but the meaning is the same; "heaven" is a Jewish paraphrase for the Divine Name.) By means of this concept it is said that salvation is not in the world, but lies in the future and comes from beyond. Side by side one observes a temporal and a spatial aspect of the kingdom, and it will not do to ignore the latter, even if the former dominates. The kingdom is, on the one hand, future; on the other hand, present. And it has a place—one "enters into" the kingdom.

That the kingdom should be near is in itself no new teaching. The Baptist had already said that (as did also the Qumran community, of course without using the concept). For the Baptist, the shortening of the time period until the end had led to a reduction in apocalyptic description and a concentration on the sense of salvation in the expected event. The call to repentance comes in the midst of eschatological

117. R. Meyer, "Eschatologie. III. Im Judentum," *RGG* 2: 662–65; H. Ringgren, "Apokalyptik. II. Jüdische," ibid. 1: 464–66.
118. H. Conzelmann, "Reich Gottes. I. Im Judentum und NT," *RGG* 5: 912–18.

preaching. With Jesus this concentration is thoroughly carried through. The difference, over against the Baptist, lies in the fact that the salvation aspect, rather than judgment, forms the point of departure. Although Jesus shares the general Jewish conception of a visible cosmic irruption of the kingdom, the "how" of its arrival does not become an independent topic in his teaching. Interest in a universal depiction (Weltbild) of the kingdom has lessened. The same is true of the future state. Jesus candidly uses the traditional images which characterize this as a state of salvation: there one celebrates the heavenly banquet (Matt. 8:11); we will be like the angels; sexual distinction disappears; since there is no more death, there is also no more marriage and procreation (Mark 12:18–27, especially v. 25). But precisely this passage shows with what critical pointedness Jesus speaks of these things. Since he says that we will be "like angels," he denies every deduction from this world to the next and at the same time criticizes indulging in fancies. Even calculation of the date is out of place; indeed the question as question is obsolete.

It is the contribution of the History-of-Religions School[119] that it pointed out the supernatural character of the kingdom of God. The kingdom is not the continuation and perfection of conditions of this world, but their end. It is not the result of a process of development; rather it breaks in suddenly from outside (Luke 17:22 ff.). It is not the result of human activity; its coming can neither be brought near nor hastened nor hindered by such. The only possibility of man's intervening in the course of events is to pray that the kingdom "come." The word "come" contains the aspects of direction (from "beyond"), suddenness,

119. J. Hempel, "Religionsgeschichtliche Schule," *RGG* 5: 991–94.

and the certainty of its arrival. It is not possible (in spite of Luke 17:21) to interpret the kingdom as a spiritual entity, as a kingdom of inwardness. It manifests itself—for Jesus, just as for Jewish apocalyptic—as a visible world transformation. The notion of "coming" in the sense of a subjective development appeals for support chiefly to the "parables of growth,"[120] in which growth in nature serves as a point of comparison (Mark 4:3–20, 26–29, 30–32, etc.). But one must not bring in the modern idea of "organic" development. On the contrary, these parables show the miraculousness of the coming. This coming is exclusively God's own work and infinitely surpasses all worldly possibilities. The present "sowing" (Jesus' own activity), to which references are made in these parables, does not mean that the kingdom is already here or is produced by Jesus (I say this against the view of Nils A. Dahl).[121] It means that the future, direct, near rule is proclaimed by Jesus in word and deed and that the eschatological salvation becomes accessible to us already now in an anticipatory way in this proclamation. The manner and method, as Jesus includes his own person in the event, is the same as in the doctrine of God and ethics. In eschatology, too, we meet with "indirect" Christology. There are still poverty, sickness, sin, demons. When the kingdom comes, there will be an end to these things. Thus it is not yet here. But it already casts its light in that it becomes operative in Jesus. Through the signs which he performs, the truth of his proclamation, the imminence of the kingdom, is guaranteed. With that,

120. N. A. Dahl, "Gleichnis und Parabel. II. In der Bibel, 3. Im NT," *RGG* 2: 1615–19, especially cols. 1618–19 (Wachstums-Gleichnisse).
121. As in note 120, and, more specifically, Dahl's article, "The Parables of Growth," *Studia Theologica* 5 (1951): 132–66.

Jesus has become the constitutive factor in eschatology.

But *how* near is the kingdom? The answers of modern research vary considerably. The kingdom of God —in the person of Jesus—"has already arrived" ("realized eschatology"; C. H. Dodd).[122] It is "in the process of realization" ("sich realisierende Eschatologie"; E. Haenchen, J. Jeremias).[123] It is future and imminently near (A. Schweitzer, R. Bultmann).[124] It is still relatively remote, since Jesus supposes that a certain time period will elapse between his ministry and the parousia. Finally, there is the view that Jesus thinks of the kingdom as "both a present and future power" (W. G. Kümmel).[125]

ii) The Results of an Examination of the Text. In this variety of hypotheses is mirrored the fact that, in the tradition, statements of different kinds stand side by side. In many sayings the kingdom appears in fact to be already present. Jesus drives out demons— *ara ephthasen eph' hymas hē basileia tou theou,* "therefore the kingdom of God has come upon you" (Matt. 12:28/Luke 11:20; cf. also Mark 3:27 par.). The kingdom is *entos hymōn,* "in your midst" (Luke 17:21). One can "receive" it (Mark 10:15), can be near it (Mark 12:34). The kingdom experiences violence in the world (Matt. 11:12). It is in such sayings

122. C. H. Dodd, *The Parables of the Kingdom* (New York: Scribner's, 1935; rev. ed. 1961).
123. J. Jeremias, *The Parables of Jesus,* trans. by S. H. Hooke (New York: Scribner's, 1954; rev. ed. 1963); see also the note on "eschatology becoming actualized" in Jeremias, *The Lord's Prayer,* trans. J. Reumann, FBBS 8 (1964), p. 32, note 27, where reference is also made to Haenchen; reprinted in *The Prayers of Jesus* (cited above, in the literature for Section 2), p. 107.
124. Schweitzer, *Quest of the Historical Jesus* (cited above, under "Research Reports" in the literature for Section 1), especially pp. 348 ff.; Bultmann, *Jesus and the Word* (cited above, under "General Presentations" in the literature for Section 1), pp. 51–52, and his *Theology* (cited above, note 76), vol. 1, pp. 4–11.
125. Kümmel, *Promise and Fulfillment* (cited above, note 70).

as these that the "realized-eschatology" interpretation finds its support. The kingdom has arrived in Jesus; a future parousia[126] is no longer to be expected. The parables of growth are understood in the same sense.

Apart from the facts that the interpretation of many of the passages cited is disputed (Luke 17:20–21; Matt. 11:12) and that the "offer" of the kingdom in sayings such as Mark 10:15 does not do away with its futurity, the kingdom appears in other passages as unequivocally future. This is the case in the announcement of its "nearness" (*engizein, engus* "draw near, [be] nigh," Mark 13:29, siding with Kümmel, against Dodd)[127]; in the concept of its "coming" (second petition of the Lord's Prayer[128]; one can still pray for it); in the expectation of "the Day" (Matt. 10:15), with which the motif of the suddenness of its arrival is connected (Matt. 24:26–27, cf. 37 ff.); and in the announcement about the future judgment. This futurity is emphasized in the parables of the Weeds and of the Fishnet (Matt. 13:24–30, 47–50). Futurity is presupposed in the insistence that the time of the coming is unknown (Mark 13:32), if this statement is authentic. The same is true of the outlook on the coming of the Son of man, if one recognizes these sayings as authentic (see Section 9b above). The formulation of the threats and promises is futuristic (Matt. 8:11; 11:11; the Beatitudes!). Because the kingdom is still not here, it is important to "watch" (Mark 13:35–37). Even the sayings about "entering" into the kingdom of God do not mean that it is already here; rather they formulate the condition for future admission into it (Windisch).[129]

126. H. Conzelmann, "Parusie," *RGG* 5: 130–32.
127. Cf. Dodd, *Parables* (cited above, note 122) pp. 44–46, and Kümmel, *Promise and Fulfillment* (cited above, note 70), pp. 19–25.
128. J. Jeremias, "Vaterunser," *RGG* 6: 1235–37.
129. Hans Windisch, "Die Sprüche von Eingehen in das Reich Gottes," *ZNW* 27 (1928): 163–92, especially 163–71.

If the point can be taken as assured, then, that one cannot reject the futuristic element, there remains the question of how long Jesus thought the time period until the arrival of the kingdom would be. The catchword *ēngiken,* "has drawn near," points to an immediate imminence; it is on the basis of this theme, indeed, that the call to repentance is established. (Even if Mark 1:14 is not a formulation of Jesus but a thematic synopsis of his preaching, it is still relevant.) Between the present call and the coming of the kingdom no time remains. On the other hand, Luke 17:22 looks to a time of affliction before the "days of the Son of man" (in accord with the familiar scheme in Jewish apocalyptic of "woes" which precede the end). Mark 14:25 reckons with a certain interval between Jesus' death and the parousia (cf. further Mark 2:18–22; Luke 13:31–35; 17:25). According to Mark 9:1 the end is still to be expected for the generation living at that time. Did Jesus then in fact reckon with a definite interim period (so Kümmel)?[130] In order to find an answer, the question of the authenticity of the sayings concerned must naturally be asked.

It is relatively easy to set aside one extensive complex of material as a construction of the church (Gemeindebildung). In this category belongs above all the apocalyptic painting in Mark 13. Here there is a combination of genuine motifs from the eschatology of Jesus (e.g., the parable of the Fig Tree, 13:28–29) with those of Jewish apocalyptic. By means of this combination there came about a comprehensive picture of the entire course of future events in history and the universe. One can readily see that the community is beginning to reckon with a delay of the parousia.[131]

130. *Promise and Fulfillment* (cited above, note 70).
131. H. Conzelmann, "Eschatologie. IV. Im Urchristentum, 7. Die Synoptiker," *RGG* 2: 671–72.

The parables form the given starting point for the reconstruction of Jesus' own view, since they contain an assured store of genuine tradition (see Section 2 above). Certainly they are painted over here and there with meanings given them by the later church, but in many cases this secondary layer is easily removed (as demonstrated by the research of Jeremias).[132] When this is done, the parables manifest a specific structure of mind toward the future: the kingdom is future, pressing near and now active in Jesus' deeds and preaching (cf. the figure of the sower).[133] This same structure is also manifested in a large number of logia, which are in the same form (J. M. Robinson).[134] The genuineness of this core of material is proved not only through indications of form but also through the content, in so far as the connection of the future expectation with the person of Jesus presumes a unique, unrepeatable situation into which the post-Easter church could no longer retroject itself without further ado.

Among the parables some are found in which the futurity of the kingdom forms precisely the point: the parables of the Weeds and of the Fishnet (Matt. 13:24–30, 47–50). No date or point in time is mentioned. (In addition to the two parables indicated above, see also the parable of the Banquet, in its original form, which is to be reconstructed by comparison of Matt. 22:1–14 and Luke 14:16–24). This lack of a date in time is not accidental. It results from the structure of the expectation. In the foreground

132. *The Parables of Jesus* (cited above, note 123).
133. See above, Section 10 d) i), p. 70.
134. *A New Quest of the Historical Jesus.* SBT 25 (1959). [Further, Robinson's "The Formal Structure of Jesus' Message," in *Current Issues in New Testament Interpretation,* ed. W. Klassen and G. F. Snyder (festschrift for Otto Piper; New York: Harper, 1962), pp. 91–110.]

stands the presentation of the value of God's rule, the salvation aspect (the parable of the Hidden Treasure in the Field, the parable of the Pearl, Matt. 13:44–46). What is found in the parable of the Talents Entrusted (Matt. 25:14–30/Luke 19:11–27) is only apparently different. In this parable there is in fact a period of time in which one has to prove himself. But this is undetermined as to its duration. That is not the point, but only a means of representing the absoluteness of the responsibility.

The meaning of the "parables of growth"[135] might lie in the fact that in them the kingdom is represented as future but that this futurity cannot be represented apocalyptically; rather, it is experienced as a present effect in the ministry of Jesus. In interpreting these parables one must include the "present" being spoken of in them and the one who is speaking (E. Fuchs).[136]

The pervading structural unity can be exhibited in terms of various themes. It can be recognized in the manner and method in which Jesus speaks of the signs of the future. At first glance, one has the impression that two groups of assertions stand in tension with each other. According to one, the kingdom comes suddenly, without any signs announcing its coming: Luke 17:20. According to the other, the signs are already here, and the question is one of understanding them: Mark 13:28–29; cf. Luke 12:54–56. There is, however, in both groups—in the assertion of suddenness and in the reference to signs—the same attitude toward the future. In both cases it is said that one cannot observe the impending kingdom as an object, with the stance of a spectator. One must grasp its

135. See above, Section 10 d) i), p. 70 and notes 120 and 121.
136. Cf. Fuchs, "Bemerkung zur Gleichnisauslegung," *ThL* 79 (1954): 345–48, and his titles listed below in the literature for Section 12.

imminence as that which determines the present. The signs are indeed of such a kind that one cannot prove them first while still meditating on them. Whoever requires signs as a means of proof receives only the sign of Jonah (Luke 11:19–20; cf. Mark 8:11–12). The genuine signs claim a person immediately and definitely. Thus the unity of both series of statements becomes intelligible in the life (Dasein) of Jesus. There is no statement about the future which would not be *eo ipso* a present definitive evaluation of "my" situation. With this, however, the question of the date of time when the kingdom arrives becomes invalid.

Radicalizing of eschatology takes place not only through contracting the time period of the interval until the end to a minimum, but also through a qualitative change. If the signs are already here and effect salvation—as healing of the blind and the lame, loosing the captives, as good news for the poor—then one cannot any more ask "when?" because the kingdom is no longer represented in a picture. The salvation of the kingdom becomes existentially intelligible to me in the present moment. I understand that on the basis of this present salvation I now can only still repent. And futurity is now no longer "not yet," but is a positive qualification of this final time, the ground of hope, and the condition for the present experience of salvation. Sayings such as Luke 17:20–21 and Mark 13:26–27 also fit in with this understanding of time. The Beatitudes correspond to this view: it is a new time, but still not the kingdom of God, because then there will be no more poor to be blessed. However, they are not put off to a future improvement of their situation. Rather their situation today is transformed —through the consolation (Zuspruche) of Jesus. The newness of this time consists therefore in the fact that it is the time of the proclamation of the kingdom (Luke 16:16; cf. Matt. 11:12–13).

It is on the basis of this conception that one will have to judge those sayings in the Synoptic tradition in which a certain delay of the parousia is delineated. They are to be regarded as a secondary development (so E. Grässer).[137]

The interpretation of the eschatology of Jesus presented here leads to the conclusion that there is no room in it for a further eschatological figure besides Jesus himself to complete the picture. Jesus did not expect another, the Son of man, as executor of universal judgment. Nor did he think either of his own future "parousia" as the Son of man. What is happening *now* is the *complete, final* announcement; only the kingdom of God itself is still to follow. Thus what was maintained above concerning the authenticity of the Son-of-man sayings (see Section 9b) is confirmed here in the concept of the kingdom of God. The figure of the Son of man is lacking in the parables and in the pointed promises of the Beatitudes. Not only is the figure lacking—there is no place at all for it here. Such a place was first found for it when—after Easter—it was necessary to draw the person of Jesus into a sketch of past, present, and future, when the church had to learn to understand itself as living in the interim period. The question of whether this transformation is theologically legitimate must be answered within the framework of the whole problematic of New Testament theology: Is the transition from the preaching *of* Jesus to the church's preaching *about* Jesus legitimate?[138]

---

137. *Das Problem der Parusieverzögerung* . . . (cited above, in the literature for Section 9).
138. [The contrast between "die Predigt Jesu" and "die Predigt der Kirche *über* Jesu" has been pointed up by Bultmann in his formula

iii) Salvation and Judgment. The pure salvific meaning of Jesus' message is also seen precisely in the fact that salvation or "eternal life"[139] is not thrown into a person's lap. Salvation demands, as its single condition, repentance. The call to repentance and the turning to the sinner are meant to be understood as a unity (H. Braun).[140] It belongs to the essence of the idea of election that the elect are a small band, an exception. Election is not something which is obvious. It is a pure gift of grace.

Thus the coming kingdom leads to separation and decision (Matt. 8:22; Luke 9:62; 14:28–33; Mark 3:35; Matt. 24:40; parables of the Weeds and the Fishnet).[141] The road into the kingdom is not wide and leads through the narrow gate (Matt. 7:13–14). The idea of judgment belongs to the idea of the kingdom with an inner logical consistency. Here, also, the general Jewish view forms the point of departure, and here again there is concentration on the fact that assertions about the judgment[142] become a determinative for the present. Through the destruction of security (*securitas*) the idea of judgment makes possible the certainty (*certitudo*) of hope.[143] It detaches the individual, an action which for the first time allows salvation to appear as something concrete, as something designated for *me*. This individualization is the prerequisite of universalism.

Jesus denies that God's future (!) judgment has al-

"the proclaimer became the proclaimed," and by earlier New Testament scholars.]

139. H. Conzelmann, "Ewiges Leben. III B. Im NT," *RGG* 2: 804–805.

140. Cf. *Radikalismus* (cited above, note 39), vol. 2, pp. 17, 29–61, 132–35.

141. See above, Section 10 d) ii), p. 74.

142. H. Conzelmann, "Gericht Gottes. III. Im NT," *RGG* 2: 1419–21.

143. H. Conzelmann, "Hoffnung. II. Im NT," *RGG* 3: 417–18.

ready been anticipated today (parable of the Weeds!), i.e., the absolute judgment of God is not replaced by an internal, moralistic judgment over man. Here too he remains consistent in proclaiming that the future is effective now. My future destiny is determined now and indeed in no other terms than my attitude toward Jesus, my obedience to his preaching.

In Jesus' presentation of the judgment there are two noticeable nuances. In one way, judgment appears as an instantaneous separation in which one is either received into the kingdom or excluded from it; it occurs in the form of a catastrophe (Matt. 11:22–24/Luke 10:14; Matt. 10:15/Luke 10:12). But alongside this it also appears as an act of judgment at which a person is judged according to his works (Matt. 12:41/Luke 11:31–32). (Again, the Son-of-man sayings form a special problem: Mark 8:38; Matt. 10:33/Luke 12:9.) In both representations, the "instantaneous" and the "forensic," the Jewish heritage is recognizable. It is used as conceptual material, as elsewhere, and it is applied here and there to show man's complete lack of security as to his own salvation.

In Jewish thinking, the idea of judgment and eternal life presumes also that of the resurrection of the dead.[144] Here Jesus shares the faith of the Pharisees regarding resurrection (cf. the question of the Sadducees, Mark 12:18–27). The destiny of blessed and of the damned is indicated in traditional images (of the heavenly banquet for the former; of hell, where fire and darkness dominate, for the latter). Jesus had no interest, however, in depicting these conditions.

iv) The Question of the Establishment of the Church. Did Jesus found a church?[145] Or did he at

---

144. H. Conzelmann, "Auferstehung. V. Im NT," *RGG* 1: 695–96.
145. K. Stendahl, "Kirche. II. Im Urchristentum," *RGG* 3: 1297–1304.

least order the founding of a church for the period after his death? Did he make the famous statement to Peter[146] (Matt. 16:17–19)? If the reconstruction of his eschatology which has been expounded here is even partially true, then all three questions must be answered in the negative. The founding of a church does not harmonize with Jesus' understanding of history. The statement to Peter is certainly old (it exhibits characteristics of Semitic speech), but it is not an authentic saying of Jesus (with Bultmann and Kümmel, against Cullmann and others).[147] The argument that to expectation of the kingdom also adheres the notion of the people of God, does not speak for, but *against,* the genuineness of the saying. For imminent expectation means that Jesus gathers the people through nothing other than his call. It is the fellowship of those who wait. Who belongs to it is connected solely with the question of whether he repents, and this will become apparent only at the judgment. Jesus does not separate this people from the rest of the world by establishing an organization. If he had intended to make the separation of the elect from the world visible organizationally, then he would not have burst asunder the framework of the Jewish sects. He issues no "rule of the community." To be sure, he calls men into his discipleship, but neither is membership in the circle of disciples a condition of salvation (see Section 8), nor is this circle closed through any institution whatsoever or ordinances.

Establishment of the church results from the appearances of the Risen One; it presupposes Jesus' death. Judgment about its legitimacy is nothing other

146. Erich Dinkler, "Petrus, Apostel," *RGG* 5: 247–49.
147. R. Bultmann, "Die Frage nach der Echtheit von Mt 16, 17–19" (cited above, in the literature for Section 9); *History of the Synoptic Tradition* (cited above, note 10), pp. 257–59; Kümmel, *Kirchenbegriff* and "Jesus und die Anfänge der Kirche" (cited above,

than judgment about the truth of the Easter faith itself. This also establishes the sense in which we can speak of institution of sacraments by "Jesus"; this matter too is connected with his death.

---

in the literature for Section 9); Oscar Cullmann, *Peter, Disciple—Apostle—Martyr: A Historical and Theological Study*, Eng. trans. by Floyd V. Filson (Philadelphia: Westminster; London: SCM, 1953), pp. 155–212; 2d rev. ed. (1962), pp. 161–217.

11

The Passion

LITERATURE FOR SECTION 11:

Lietzmann, Hans. *Der Prozess Jesu.* Sitzungsberichte der Preussischen Akademie der Wissenschaften zu Berlin 1931. Pp. 313–22.

———. "Bemerkungen zum Prozess Jesu." *ZNW* 30 (1931): 211–15.

Dibelius, Martin. "Das historische Problem der Leidensgeschichte." Ibid., pp. 193–201. Reprinted in his collected essays, *Botschaft und Geschichte* (cited above, literature for Section 5), 1 (1953), pp. 248–57.

Macaulay, A. B. *The Death of Jesus.* London: Hodder and Stoughton, 1938.

Schelkle, K. H. *Die Passion Jesu in der Verkündigung des Neuen Testaments.* Heidelberg: Kerle, 1949.

Blinzler, Josef. *Der Prozess Jesu: Das jüdische und das römische Gerichtsverfahren gegen Jesus Christus auf Grund der ältesten Zeugnisse dargestellt und beurteilt.* Regensburg: Pustet, 1951; 2d ed. 1955 (includes bibliography). Eng. trans. by Isabel and Florence McHugh, *The Trial of Jesus: The Jewish and Roman Proceedings against Jesus Christ Described and Assessed from the Oldest Accounts.* Cork, Ireland: Mercier Press; Westminster, Maryland: Newman Press, 1959.

———. "Der Entscheid des Pilatus: Exekutionsbefehl oder Todesurteil?" *Münchener Theologische Zeitschrift* 5 (1954): 171–94.

Knox, John. *The Death of Jesus: The Cross in New Testament History and Faith.* New York: Abingdon, 1958.

Burkill, T. A. "The Trial of Jesus." *Vigiliae Christianae* 12 (1958): 1–18. Reprinted, with revisions, in Burkill's *Mysterious Revelation: An Examination of the Philosophy of St. Mark's Gospel.* Ithaca, N. Y.: Cornell University Press, 1963. Pp. 280–299.

THE PASSION STORY is the portion of the Synoptic tradition which first assumed a fixed form.[148] It is completely and totally formed from the perspective of the Easter faith. This provides the key for the interpretation of Jesus' death. The narrative is thus permeated throughout by christological motifs, particularly in the story of the entry into Jerusalem, the Last Supper, and the trial before the Sanhedrin. The first is formed into a legend with epiphany motifs. The report of the institution of the Lord's Supper[149] in its present form is a cult legend, a *hieros logos* of the celebration of the Christian sacrament. At first the report of the trial gives the impression of being historical, but analysis of it shows that the church possessed no eyewitness report of the trial. The church shaped the course of events as it conceived them. It was natural, when looking at the whole matter in retrospect, that the assumption would be that the main point of the proceedings had been the messiahship of Jesus. Thus this forms the center of the entire trial. At the climactic point of the trial it is pointed out—for the Christian reader!—with forceful formulation how Jesus, before the supreme authorities of his people, for the first time explicitly acknowledges that he is the messiah—and thereby brings about his own death. At the same time this discloses the unbelief of Israel.

Scriptural proof shapes the account more strongly in the passion narrative than in the other parts of the gospels (noted by Dibelius).[150] Entire motifs, indeed entire scenes (e.g., Jesus before Herod, Luke 23:6–16)

148. G. Bornkamm, "Evangelien, formgeschichtlich," *RGG* 2: 752.
149. E. Schweizer, "Abendmahl. I. Im NT," *RGG* 1: 10–21. Eng. trans. cited above (note 48).
150. M. Dibelius, "Das historische Problem der Leidensgeschichte" (cited above, in the literature for Section 11); cf. also his book, *From Tradition to Gospel* (cited above, note 10), pp. 184–89.

are created out of Old Testament texts. This is the derivation also of the saying which is placed on Jesus' lips as he is dying: "My God, my God, why have you forsaken me?" (Psalm 22:2 = Mark 15:34). The objection that this saying would not have been put into his mouth if Jesus had not actually said it fails to recognize the character of the narrative. If one took up this saying, he then showed that the death of Jesus was a fulfillment and thereby overcame the scandal of the cross. A person thus may not evaluate the saying psychologically in order to reconstruct the feelings of Jesus as he was dying.

In spite of the christological motifs in the passion history, an original historical element can, admittedly, be recognized. At several places there may still be traces of an eyewitness report (e.g., Mark 14:51; 15:21, 40?). It must be conceded that the length of Jesus' stay in Jerusalem has not been established. According to Mark, everything happened in a week, but this is a redactional scheme. In any case, it is more certain that Jesus went to Jerusalem[151] in order to place before his people in their very center, at the place of the temple and of the highest authorities, a final decision. Naturally his appearance must have been interpreted by the leadership of the people as an attack on the foundations of religion and the nation. So, just as it is narrated, they seized him with the aid of one of the disciples (Judas Iscariot)[152] and handed him over to the Roman procurator, Pontius Pilate,[153] who at that particular time was residing in the city. It is established that Jesus was executed by the Romans (and not by the Jews) since crucifixion is a Roman form of

151. On Jerusalem as a place, cf. F. Maass, "Jerusalem. III. Heilige Stätten," *RGG* 3: 596–97.
152. E. Fascher, "Judas Iskarioth," *RGG* 3: 965–66.
153. E. Bammel, "Pilatus, Pontius," *RGG* 5: 383–84.

capital punishment and not a Jewish one. For the question of the date (Nisan 14 or 15), see Section 4, above.

The most vigorously disputed historical problem is whether the Sanhedrin at that time possessed competency as a criminal court and, if it did, to what extent. (1) Did it have the right to impose the death penalty (Lietzmann)?[154] Or, (2) if it did pronounce such a sentence, was it necessary for this judgment to be ratified by the Roman procurator (as Dibelius held)?[155] Or (3) was the Sanhedrin required, as a general practice, to surrender jurisdiction over all capital proceedings to the procurator? In the last-mentioned case, the interrogation of Jesus before this Jewish court would not have been a legal proceeding resulting in a decision, but would have had a fact-finding character. If the second possibility mentioned above were the case, the Jewish court, rather than Pilate, would have passed the sentence, and Pilate would merely have given the order for execution. If the first case were true, there is then the question of why the Sanhedrin turned Jesus over to the Romans at all. Lietzmann took the position that the Sanhedrin did possess the *ius gladii* (power of the sword) and concluded from that—a conclusion in itself consistent—that the report of the trial before the Sanhedrin is not historical. Now the method of execution ought itself to prove that Pilate pronounced the death sentence and did not simply give the command for execution. The inconsistency which exists in the fact that then two trials = legal proceedings stand alongside each other is removed through awareness of the literary character of the report. It is indeed a report which was drawn

154. *Der Prozess Jesu* and other titles cited above in the literature for Section 11.
155. As cited above, in the literature for Section 11 and in note 150.

up only subsequent to the events and drawn up on the basis of concepts of Christians. It is this christological interest which dominates in the account. There was scarcely any feeling of accountability for legal detail and judicial plausibility. According to the view of the Synoptic narrative, both the Sanhedrin and Pilate condemned Jesus.

One special subject of discussion, finally, is the fact that the report on the trial of Jesus does not correspond to Jewish criminal procedure presented in the Mishnah,[156] Tractate Sanhedrin. In order to remove the discrepancy there are three major possibilities. One could assume that the interrogation of Jesus was not an actual criminal case. Secondly one could assume that the stipulations were ignored at the trial of Jesus. Or one could assume that the Sanhedrin regulations (of the Mishnah) had at that time not yet been put in force (so Josef Blinzler).[157] The third possibility is doubtless the correct one: what we have in the court rules of the Mishnah is an ideal construction. Beyond this, however, one must maintain that in all attempts to reconstruct the actual course of events there are many unknown factors, since we possess no minutes of the trial. Methodologically it is misleading to interpret the present report as such a record. It is a witness of faith.

156. E. Gross, "Mischna," *RGG* 4: 966–68.
157. *The Trial of Jesus,* cited above in the literature for Section 11.

12

The Historical Jesus and Faith
(Jesus of Nazareth and Jesus Christ)

LITERATURE FOR SECTION 12:

Fuchs, Ernst. "Jesu Selbstzeugnis nach Mt 5." *ZThK* 51 (1952): 14–34. Reprinted in *Zur Frage nach dem historischen Jesus*. Tübingen: Mohr, 1960. Pp. 100–25.

———. *Hermeneutik*. Bad Cannstatt: Müllerschön, 1954; 2d ed. 1958.

———. "Die Frage nach dem historischen Jesus." *ZThK* 53 (1956): 210–29. Reprinted in *Zur Frage nach dem historischen Jesus* (cited above), pp. 143–67. Eng. trans. by Andrew Scobie, "The Quest of the Historical Jesus," in Fuch's *Studies of the Historical Jesus*. SBT 42 (1964). Pp. 11–31.

———. "Glaube und Geschichte im Blick auf die Frage nach dem historischen Jesus." *ZThK* 54 (1957): 117–56. Reprinted in *Zur Frage nach dem historischen Jesus* (cited above), pp. 168–218.

———. "Jesus und der Glaube." *ZThK* 55 (1958): 170–85. Reprinted in *Zur Frage nach dem historischen Jesus* (cited above), pp. 238–57. Eng. trans. by Andrew Scobie, "Jesus and Faith," in Fuchs's *Studies of the Historical Jesus* (cited above), pp. 48–64.

Käsemann, Ernst. "Das Problem des historischen Jesus." *ZThK* 51 (1954): 125–53. Reprinted in *Exegetische Versuche und Besinnungen*. Vol. 1. Göttingen: Vandenhoeck & Ruprecht, 1960. Pp. 187–214. Eng. trans. by W. J. Montague, "The Problem of the Historical Jesus," in Käsemann's *Essays on New Testament Themes*. SBT 41 (1964). Pp. 15–47.

Dahl, N. A. "Der historische Jesus als geschichtswissenschaftliches und theologisches Problem." *Kerygma und Dogma* 1 (1955): 104–32.

Heitsch, E. "Die Aporie des historischen Jesus als Problem theologischer Hermeneutik." *ZThK* 53 (1956): 192–210.

Biehl, P. "Zur Frage nach dem historischen Jesus." *Theologische Rundschau* NF 24 (1956–57): 54–76.

Diem, Hermann. *Der irdische Jesus und der Christus des Glaubens.* Sammlung gemeinverständlicher Vorträge und Schriften aus dem Gebiet der Theologie und Religionsgeschichte 215. Tübingen: Mohr. 1957.

Mussner, F. "Der historische Jesus und der Christus des Glaubens." *Biblische Zeitschrift* NF 1 (1957): 257–75.

Schneider, J. *Die Frage nach dem historischen Jesus in der neutestamentlichen Forschung der Gegenwart.* Berlin: Evangelische Verlagsanstalt, 1958.

Ebeling, Gerhard. "Jesus und Glaube." *ZThK* 55 (1958): 64–110. Reprinted in *Wort und Glaube.* Vol. 1. Tübingen: Mohr, 1962. Pp. 203–54. Eng. trans. by J. W. Leitch, "Jesus and Faith," in Ebeling's *Word and Faith.* Philadelphia: Fortress, 1963. Pp. 201–46.

Jeremias, Joachim. "The Present Position in the Controversy concerning the Problem of the historical Jesus." *Expository Times* 69 (1958): 333–39. Rev. trans. by Norman Perrin, *The Problem of the Historical Jesus,* FBBS 13 (1964, rev. ed. 1969) (bibliography).

Robinson, James M. *A New Quest of the Historical Jesus.* SBT 25 (1959).

a) IN TERMS OF historical presentation, what happens after the crucifixion of Jesus is no longer the history of Jesus but the history of its consequences. Even though this area also belongs to the history of a personality and determines our relationship to him (which itself is a historical relationship), still in principle Jesus is in this respect like other historical figures. Even a unique consequence cannot justify an *absolute* claim. And if Jesus himself raises such an absolute claim, then its validity cannot be decided through historical inquiry.

Rudolf Bultmann[158] has formulated the problem

158. E. Fuchs, "Bultmann, Rudolf," *RGG* 1: 1511–12.

most clearly in his two slogans—"demythologizing"[159] and "existential interpretation." Insofar as Jesus is a possible object of existential interpretation, he is, of course, isolated as a phenomenon of history, and one tries to comprehend him in his individuality. In principle, however, he "encounters" a person the same way as any other historical phenomenon. This goes for his death also, which can be interpreted, e.g., analogously to the death of Socrates. The theological question can be stated thus: How can a historical event be the *eschatological* event and encounter a person as such today? The answer is to be given by referring to proclamation: it can be present when *preached*. This possibility is then to be distinguished on principle from the historically comprehensible consequences of a personality.

Now precisely in this framing of the question, further historical inquiry is not opposed, but is required. However, it no longer has as its aim that of giving faith its content—that it receives through preaching.[160] Rather its purpose is to keep us from losing sight of the historicity of the revelation and to confirm the fact that revelation[161] is not a body of teaching, but a historical and historically encountered act. In dogmatic terms, this means that the belief that Jesus is true man is a tenet of faith which must be concretized time and again. The historical reference must, therefore, constantly be kept in mind, without one's postulating historical facts of content from faith which is presumed. Thus historical investigation as such acquires a definite relevance for theology. This

159. H. Ott, "Entmythologisierung," *RGG* 2: 496–99.
160. A. Niebergall et al., "Predigt," *RGG* 5: 516–39, especially M. Doerne, "II. Grundsätzliches," cols. 530–34.
161. C.-M. Edsman et al., "Offenbarung," *RGG* 4: 1597–1613, especially O. A. Piper, "IV. Im NT," cols. 1603–1605, and G. Gloege, "VI. Christliche Offenbarung, dogmatisch," cols. 1609–13.

relevance nevertheless is not to be stipulated in general theses about faith and history. It must itself be made concrete again and again. Maintaining the historical reference opposes the mythologizing of the object of faith as well as dogmatic objectivizing in which a series of statements about him takes the place of Jesus Christ. Statements cannot be an object of faith but only its explication.

b) The fact that the relationship of Jesus the preacher to the Christ who is preached has generally become a problem, indeed the central problem, of New Testament theology presupposes the origin of modern historical consciousness and, as a result of that, consideration of the biblical texts as historical sources.[162] Since then, it is simply present as a problem which must be stated as such and not denied or deplored. In order to escape the problem, two ways have been suggested. The first proposes that one can refer faith to the result of historical reconstruction, thus to the "historical Jesus" or at least to his teaching. This is the program of the classical "life-of-Jesus theology." It is carried along by the optimistic conviction that a unanimous result is attainable. This position fails to recognize, for one thing, that the relationship to history is itself historical (something which could not in any way be understood relativistically). For another thing, there is the conviction that through historical reconstruction it is possible to discover truth, truth which itself is no longer to be grounded historically. History is here understood as the history of the effect of a great personality or a history of ideas; and faith is understood as the acceptance of a religio-ethical world view or of a view of history. The biblical texts, of course, may be uti-

162. W. G. Kümmel, "Bibelwissenschaft. II. Bibelwissenschaft des NT," *RGG* 1: 1236–51.

lized as sources, but are lost as *text*. The drawback is that modern presuppositions must be slipped in unnoticed, in order to show a present meaning for this reconstruction.

The second and contrary possibility, in order to avoid the impasse, argues that this reconstruction of Jesus is in no way binding for faith. Indeed it is stated that—on the basis of an examination of the sources—such reconstruction is not at all possible (Martin Kähler).[163] The text remains text. Faith is not exposed to the vicissitudes of scholarly results; it is founded on the "witness to Christ of the gospels." This program of renouncing further inquiry behind the Easter event and the church's preaching of Jesus as the Christ appeals, among other things, to the results of form criticism. For form criticism causes the amount of material available for a "life of Jesus" to dwindle very considerably and shows, on the other hand, that the gospels[164] are intended to be read not as historical sources, but as witnesses of faith. There is a short circuit here, however, in the fact that it is concluded from this that the gospels cannot and should not be used as sources. Whether the texts yield historical results can be determined only through critical analysis.

There must be a clear distinction made between the understanding of history in the gospels[165] and our contemporary historical consciousness. Just as surely as we try to clarify this in the historical material, just so certainly we cannot take over the historical consciousness of that time. Generally it does not lie in the realm of possible human resolve (Entschluss). And if it were

163. R. Hermann, "Kähler, Martin," *RGG* 3: 1081–84.
164. G. Bornkamm, "Evangelien," *RGG* 2: 749–66.
165. Erich Dinkler, "Geschichte und Geschichtsauffassung. II. Christliche, A. Neutestamentlich, 4. Synoptiker . . . ," *RGG* 2: 1478–79.

possible to take this over, it would have nothing to do with faith. Fundamentally, both of the attempts at a solution to this problem mentioned above—the first (or Liberal) and second (or biblicistic or dialectic)—rest upon an analogous objectivizing of the content of faith. In both cases the authority of the content of faith is said to be ascertained directly. This is so, really, even in the second case because of the sort of historicizing viewpoint which results—only not exactly of a person, but of a historically available "witness." But its validity is authenticated nowhere else than in contemporary proclamation (Herman Diem).[166]

In light of these common foundations, one understands the "exchange of fronts" (Ernst Käsemann's phrase)[167] which is characteristic of the present situation among scholars. The "historians" have seen themselves forced to make further inquiry about the kerygma,[168] and those on the other side ask about the historical Jesus or his teaching as the foundation of present faith. Thus we are threatened with a repetition of the old impasse. On the one side it is stated that authority cannot be founded in this way. On the other side it is said that "a historical truth, in contrast to one that is generally valid, cannot be repeated without change" and that the words and deeds of Jesus cannot be "brought into the present" without further ado (Ernst Fuchs). Theologically, every result of the reconstruction of the life of Jesus is considered as law, not gospel. From this fact not only its limits, but also its claim is determined.

166. *Der irdische Jesus und der Christus des Glaubens* (cited above, in the literature for Section 12).
167. E. Käsemann, "The Problem of the Historical Jesus" (German originally in *ZThK* 51 [1954], pp. 125–53), Eng. trans. by W. J Montague, *Essays on New Testament Themes,* SBT 41 (1964), p. 17.
168. H. Ott, "Kerygma," *RGG* 3: 1250–54.

c) For historical consideration the question poses itself simply as that of the transition from Jesus' own ministry to the gathering of his followers under the impact of the appearances of the Risen One[169] and to the formation of faith in him as the messiah and Son of God.[170] It can be shown how this faith developed into a critical principle for selection of material. One part of the available material—naturally not by conscious reflection—was rejected, e.g., the recollection of Jesus' human personality, what he looked like, his character. Another part was taken up into the meaning of faith. In connection with the latter, the question must be raised as to the extent to which the material on its part influenced the development—not of faith, but—of the conception of faith.

To what extent, then, can continuity between Jesus and the community of believers be shown? In its own understanding, the church takes for granted that the Risen One is the Crucified One; the Risen One is firmly held to be none other than the man Jesus of Nazareth. This is true for both basic types of New Testament Christology.[171] It is true in Hellenistic-Pauline Christology, where the historical material from the life of Jesus is ignored (2 Cor. 5:16)—up to the *punctum mathematicum* of his having existed. It also is true in the Synoptic gospels, where faith is illustrated through a collection of remembered material. Thus, according to the church's understanding, Jesus himself remains the presupposition of faith. This, then, prevents mythologizing the figure of the Redeemer. In addition, the continuity can be shown from the other direction, from Jesus to the church,

169. H. Conzelmann, "Auferstehung Christi. I. Im NT," *RGG* 1: 698–700.
170. Bultmann, *Theology* (cited above, note 76), vol. 1, pp. 33 ff.
171. G. Sevenster, "Christologie. I. Christologie des Urchristentums, *RGG* 1: 1745–62.

since his call to decision—even without *direct* christological assertions—really implies a Christology (Rudolf Bultmann).[172]

The lines cross at the point of the resurrection. This is regarded by the church as an event in space and time (cf. the list of witnesses in 1 Cor. 15:3 ff.). Of course, the church did not reflect about the relationship of the historical and suprahistorical. It is also the case here that we simply cannot reach back to the early church's conceptions. As soon as reflection is there, the process cannot be made reversible; the reflection must be sustained. This shows that history cannot establish the facticity of the resurrection. It can only establish that men testified that they had seen Jesus alive after his death. In this experience they find the key for the meaning of his death. This interpretation is not only carried out in the formulation of doctrinal statements and confessional formulas,[173] but it becomes specific also in the fact that the church knows itself to be established through the death of him who is now its Lord (cf. the words of institution of the Lord's Supper).[174] With this the assertion that the resurrection is not a historical event must be adhered to quite clearly. This assertion implies that theology can postulate no historical facts (Tatsachen) and does not need to do so, since it lives by proclamation. On the other hand, it implies that the church cannot altogether interpret historical research disinterestedly by constricting itself to a witness of faith. Otherwise the result is the fatal consequence that this witness becomes the object of faith (see above), and faith would then mean accepting a historical fact as

172. *Theology* (cited above, note 76), vol. 1, p. 43.
173. E. Käsemann, "Formeln. II. Liturgische Formeln im NT, 5. Bekenntnis-Formeln," *RGG* 2: 995.
174. E. Schweizer, "Abendmahl. I. Im NT," and Eng. trans. (cited above, note 48).

true on the basis of someone else's faith. Faith would then have become a matter of human resolve (Entschluss), and thus a "work." That is the price which must be paid for demonstrating the object of faith. Precisely ● view of the witness to the resurrection, we must maintain that the object of faith appears only to faith itself. Revelation is not "facts laid out before a person"; it emerges—today—in the word.

The denial of any historical objectivizing of the resurrection by no means implies its dissolution into a psychic phenomenon, viz., the experience of visionaries. Rather it precisely enables one to overcome the difficult alternative of "subjective-objective." The objective givenness of the resurrection itself before faith is simply and solely an insight of faith itself which understands that it is founded upon the resurrection as sola gratia.

If the object of faith is not subjectively, intuitively evident as such, then the relationship of faith to the historical Jesus can only be a specific punctiliar one. The single historical fixed point is in fact the naked "that" (dass) of the existence (Dagewesensein) of Jesus (in agreement with Bultmann).[175] Only then can it be shown how a historical event (Jesus' death, or in Pauline terms, the cross) can be preached. It has already been pointed out that this does not cut off further historical inquiry. Rather it is a matter of referring this inquiry to its correct theological place. This becomes intelligible when I learn to distinguish myself as spectator of world history from myself as

175. In addition to Bultmann's *Jesus and the Word* (cited above, under "General Presentations," literature for Section 1) and his writings generally, see especially his address to the Heidelberg Academy in 1959, stating his views on the New Quest, that only the *dass* matters and is accessible (the fact *that* Jesus existed), not the *was* (*what* he was like). Eng. trans. in *The Historical Jesus and the Kerygmatic Christ* (cited below, in the supplementary bibliography for Section 12, under "For Further Reading").

hearer of the proclamation without thereby splitting myself in two. As the spectator which I always already am, I am addressed.

Only if one includes the event of proclamation in the problematic does he avoid the risk which today, as ever, threatens, viz., that once again in our day a picture of Jesus is made the basis of faith, a picture which is again psychologically based. The corresponding misunderstanding lies close at hand precisely in some of the recent formulations: "Jesus and faith" (Ebeling), or "Jesus and the faith" (Fuchs), or the thesis that the conduct of Jesus implies a Christology (Fuchs).[176] For these formulizations would be illegitimate if Jesus' present claim were once again directly derived from the psychological self-consciousness of Jesus. It comes down to a question of whether our historical relationship to Jesus is to be made binding in the sense of the influence of his person, or in the sense of the continuity of the history of the church, which is not to be understood as a history of ideas (geistesgeschichtlich) but means continuity with respect to the text which is to be interpreted (Ebeling). Then one can in fact state that Jesus himself is the presupposition of Christology, and this in turn becomes a "doctrine of the Word of God which does not lose sight of the historical Jesus" (Fuchs).

176. For the views alluded to in this paragraph, see the literature cited above for Section 12: Ebeling, "Jesus and Faith"; Fuchs, "Jesus und der Glaube," Eng. trans. by Andrew Scobie, "Jesus and Faith," in *Studies of the Historical Jesus,* SBT 42 (1964). The final phrase quoted above is from Fuchs's essay, "The Quest of the Historical Jesus," in *Studies,* SBT 42, p. 31: "The dogmatic continuation of exegetical analysis would have to be a doctrine of the word of God which keeps its sights firmly trained on the historical Jesus."

For Further Reading

BIBLIOGRAPHY OF THE WRITINGS OF
HANS CONZELMANN:

(Books and major articles, arranged chronologically; where a summary appears in *New Testament Abstracts*, it is noted by a reference to *NT Abstracts*, the volume and item number.)

Die Mitte der Zeit: Studien zur Theologie des Lukas. Beiträge zur historischen Theologie 17. Tübingen: Mohr, 1954; 2d ed. 1957; 3d rev. ed. 1960. Eng. trans. by G. Buswell, *The Theology of St Luke.* New York; Harper; London, Faber & Faber, 1960.

Die kleineren Briefe des Apostels Paulus. Das Neue Testament Deutsch, 8. 9th ed. Göttingen: Vandenhoeck & Ruprecht, 1962. Conzelmann provided new commentaries on Colossians and Ephesians in this popular series.

Die Apostelgeschichte. Handbuch zum Neuen Testament 7. Tübingen: Mohr, 1963.

Die Pastoralbriefe by Martin Dibelius. Handbuch zum Neuen Testament 13. 4th ed. Tübingen: Mohr, 1966. Eng. trans. by Philip Buttolph and Adela Yarbro, *The Pastoral Epistles.* Ed. Helmut Koester. Hermeneia—A Critical and Historical Commentary on the Bible. Philadelphia: Fortress, 1971. This volume represents Conzelmann's revisions of Dibelius's work.

Grundriss der Theologie des Neuen Testaments. Einführung in die evangelische Theologie, vol. 2. Munich: Chr. Kaiser, 1967. Eng. trans. by J. Bowden, *An Outline of the Theology of the New Testament.* New York: Harper & Row, 1969.

Der erste Brief an die Korinther. Kritisch-exegetischer Kommentar über das Neue Testament, 5. 11th ed. Göttingen: Vandenhoeck & Ruprecht, 1969.

Geschichte des Urchristentums. Grundrisse zum Neuen Testament, Das Neue Testament Deutsch Ergänzungsreihe, vol. 5. Göttingen: Vandenhoeck & Ruprecht, 1969.

Articles in *Theologisches Wörterbuch zum Neuen Testament,* ed. G. Kittel and G. Friedrich. Stuttgart: Kohlhammer. Eng. trans. by G. W. Bromiley, *Theological Dictionary of the New Testament.* Grand Rapids: Eerdmans. (Dates and pages are given in parentheses): *"skotos,* etc." ("darkness"), vol. 7 (1964), pp. 424–46 (Eng., 1971, pp. 423–45); *"syniēmi, synesis,* etc." ("bring together," "union"), 7, pp. 886–94 (Eng., pp. 888–96).

Articles in *RGG* 3d ed.:

"Amt. II. Im NT," 1: 335–37; "Auferstehung. V. Im NT," 1: 695–96; "Auferstehung Christi. I. Im NT," 1: 698–700; "Eschatologie. IV. Im Urchristentum," 2: 665–72; "Ewiges Leben. III B. Im NT," 2: 804–805; "Gericht Gottes. III. Im NT," 2: 1419–21; "Heidenchristentum," 3: 128–41; "Hoffnung. II. Im NT," 3: 417–18; "Parusie," 5: 130–32; "Reich Gottes. I. Im Judentum und NT," 5: 912–18; "Zorn Gottes. III. Im Judentum und NT," 6: 1931–32.

"Gegenwart und Zukunft in der synoptischen Tradition." *ZThK* 54 (1957): 277–96. Eng. trans, "Present and Future in the Synoptic Tradition," in *Journal for Theology and the Church* (cited above, in the literature for Section 9) 5 (1968): 26–44. *NT Abstracts,* 13: 551.

"Geschichte und Eschaton nach Mc 13." *ZNW* 50 (1959): 210–21. *NT Abstracts* 4: 661.

"Zur Methode der Leben-Jesu-Forschung." *ZThK* 56 (1959): 2–13. *NT Abstracts* 5: 10. Eng. trans. by C. E. Braaten and R. A. Harrisville, eds. *The Historical Jesus and the Kerygmatic Christ: Essays on the New Quest of the Historical Jesus.* Nashville & New York: Abingdon, 1964). Pp. 54–68.

"Geschichte, Geschichtsbild und Geschichtsdarstellung bei Lukas." *ThL* 85 (1960): 241–50. *NT Abstracts* 5: 896r. Review of Haenchen's commentary on Acts.

"Randbemerkungen zur Lage im 'Neuen Testament.'" *Evangelische Theologie* 22 (1962): 225–33. *NT Abstracts* 7: 412.

"Jesu självmedvetande." *Svensk Exegetisk Arsbok* 28–29

(1963–64): 39–53. *NT Abstracts* 10: 72. On Jesus' self-consciousness.

"Fragen an Gerhard von Rad." *Evangelische Theologie* 24 (1964): 113–25. *NT Abstracts* 9: 4.

"Theologie und Positivismus." In *Positivismus als wissenschaftstheoretisches Problem.* Ed. P. Schneider and O. Saame. Mainzer Universitätsgespräche Wintersemester 1964/65.

"Zur Analyse der Bekenntnisformel I. Kor. 15, 3–5." *Evangelische Theologie* 25 (1965): 1–11. *NT Abstracts* 9: 1009. Eng. trans., "On the Analysis of the Confessional Formula in I Corinthians 15: 3–5." *Interpretation* 20 (1966): 15–25.

"Paulus und die Weisheit." *New Testament Studies* 12 (1965–66): 231–44. *NT Abstracts* 11: 330.

"Luke's Place in the Development of Early Christianity." *Studies in Luke-Acts. Essays presented in honor of Paul Schubert.* Ed. L. E. Keck and J. L. Martyn. Nashville & New York: Abingdon, 1966. Pp. 298–316.

"The Address of Paul on the Areopagus." Ibid. Pp. 217–30.

"The First Christian Century: As Christian History." In *The Bible in Modern Scholarship* (Society of Biblical Literature Centenary Papers). Ed. J. P. Hyatt. Nashville & New York: Abingdon, 1966. Pp. 217–26.

"Jesu Wirken nach seinem Tod." In *Die Zeit Jesu.* Ed. H. J. Schultz. *Kontexte,* vol. 3. Stuttgart and Berlin: Kreuz-Verlag, 1966. Pp. 119–24. Eng. trans. by Brian Watchorn. "The Influence of Jesus after his Death." In *Jesus in His Time.* Philadelphia: Fortress, 1971. Pp. 142–48.

"Current Problems in Pauline Research." *Interpretation* 22 (1968): 171–86. *NT Abstracts* 12: 947. German original in *Der Evangelische Erzieher* 18 (1966): 241–52.

"Historie und Theologie in den synoptischen Passionsberichten." In *Zur Bedeutung des Todes Jesu: Evangelische Beiträge.* Schriftenreihe des Theologischen Ausschusses der Evangelischen Kirche der Union. Gütersloh: Gerd Mohn, 1967. Pp. 35–54. Eng. trans., "History and Theology in the Passion Narratives of the Synoptic Gospels." *Interpretation* 24 (1970): 178–97. *NT Abstracts* 15: 117.

"Auslegung von Markus 4, 35–41 par.; Markus, 8, 31–37 par.; Römer 1, 3f." *Der Evangelische Erzieher* 20 (1968); 249–60. *NT Abstracts* 13:193.

"Die Rechtfertigungslehre des Paulus: Theologie oder Anthropologie?" *Evangelische Theologie* 28 (1968): 389–404. *NT Abstracts* 13: 637.

"Zum Überlieferungsproblem im Neuen Testament." *ThL* 94 (1969): 881–88. *NT Abstracts* 15: 3.

"Thèmes et tendances de l'exégèse du Nouveau Testament en Allemagne." *Études théologiques et religieuses* (Montpellier) 46 (1971): 429–43. *NT Abstracts* 16: 428.

ABOUT THE SUBJECT OF THIS BOOK
(selected titles, chiefly since 1959, supplementing Professor Conzelmann's bibliography, arranged according to the sections above):

1. Motifs in Life-of-Jesus Research:
General Presentations:

ANDERSON, CHARLES C. *Critical Quests of Jesus.* Grand Rapids: Eerdmans, 1969.

———. *The Historical Jesus: A Continuing Quest.* Grand Rapids: Eerdmans, 1972. These two titles analyze past efforts and take up current problems from a more conservative point of view.

ANDERSON, HUGH. *Jesus and Christian Origins: A Commentary on Modern Viewpoints.* New York: Oxford University Press, 1964. A helpful survey, with mediating insights of its own.

BARRETT, C. K. *Jesus and the Gospel Tradition.* London: SPCK, 1967; Philadelphia: Fortress, 1968. How Jesus taught about and looked upon his death and the future.

BOWMAN, JOHN WICK. *Which Jesus?* Philadelphia: Westminster, 1970. Classifies "lives" of Jesus over the last half century into seven types.

GRANT, ROBERT M. *The Earliest Lives of Jesus.* New York: Harper; London: SPCK, 1961. Evidence from the church fathers on interest in the "quest" during the patristic period.

————. "The Problem of the Life of Jesus." In his *Historical Introduction to the New Testament.* New York: Harper; London: Collins, 1963. Pp. 284–377. Professor Grant's analysis of the subsequent "quest" and the current situation, for the beginning student.

GRECH, P. "Recent Developments in the Jesus of History Controversy." *Biblical Theology Bulletin* 1 (1971): 190–213. *NT Abstracts* 16: 90.

HARVEY, VAN A. *The Historian and the Believer: The Morality of Historical Knowledge and Christian Belief.* New York: Macmillan, 1966. Especially pp. 164–203. Sets the quest in the larger context of faith and historical methods.

JEREMIAS, JOACHIM. *The Problem of the Historical Jesus.* Eng. trans. by N. Perrin. FBBS 13 (1964, rev. ed. 1969). Bibliography, pp. 25–27. Sets forth Jeremias's oft-expressed view that the historical Jesus is God's revelation, to which the kerygma is the church's response.

KECK, LEANDER E. *A Future for the Historical Jesus: The Place of Jesus in Preaching and Theology.* Nashville & New York: Abingdon, 1971.

KÜMMEL, W. G. "Jesusforschung seit 1950." *Theologische Rundschau* NF 31 (1966): 15–46, 289–315. Research report on selected "lives" and studies.

LÉON-DUFOUR, XAVIER, S. J. *Les évangiles et l'histoire de Jésus.* Paris, Éditions du Seuil, 1963. Eng. trans. by John McHugh. *The Gospels and the Jesus of History.* New York & Tournai: Desclée; London: Collins, 1968. Garden City: Doubleday, Image Books; London: Fontana Books, 1970. The English is an abbreviated version of a French Catholic approach to the gospels and the historical Jesus.

McARTHUR, HARVEY K. *The Quest Through the Centuries: The Search for the Historical Jesus.* Philadelphia: Fortress, 1966. Selected segments of life-of-Jesus study from ancient to modern times.

NINEHAM, D. E. "Some Reflections on the Present Position with Regard to the Jesus of History." *Church Quarterly Review* 166 (1965): 5–21. Reprinted in *Historicity and Chronology in the New Testament* (cited below, Section 4), pp. 1–18.

PERRIN, NORMAN. *Rediscovering the Teaching of Jesus.*

New York: Harper & Row, 1967. The methodology developed, the exegesis of passages, and the annotated bibliography (pp. 249–66) show how form and redaction criticism work.

SCHWEIZER, EDUARD. "Die Frage nach dem historischen Jesus." *Evangelische Theologie* 24 (1964): 403–19. For the outcome of Schweizer's approach to the problem, see his *Jesus,* cited under "Lives" in the next section below.

VÖGTLE, ANTON. "Jesus Christus." *Lexikon für Theologie und Kirche.* 2d ed. Freiburg: Herder. Vol. 5 (1960), cols. 922–32. Survey article for German Roman Catholic encyclopedia similar to the Protestant *RGG,* by a scholar who endorses the critical-historical method, but subject to standards of the pre-Vatican II period.

ZAHRNT, HEINZ. *Es begann mit Jesus von Nazareth: Die Frage nach dem historischen Jesus.* Stuttgart: Kreuz-Verlag, 1960. Eng. trans. by J. S. Bowden. *The Historical Jesus.* New York: Harper & Row; London: Collins, 1963. A very readable summary of the last century of the "quest," especially its more recent trends.

See also *Interpretation* 16,2 (April, 1962): 131–92, and the *Journal of Bible and Religion* 30,2 (July, 1962): 198–223, which are devoted to the "new quest." Further literature on the new quest is cited in Section 12 below.

"Lives" of Jesus:

BEN-CHORIN, S. *Bruder Jesus: Der Nazarener in jüdischer Sicht.* Munich: Paul List Verlag, 1967; 3d ed., 1970.

BETZ, OTTO. *Was wissen wir von Jesu?* Stuttgart: Kreuz-Verlag, 1965. Eng. trans. by Margaret Kohl. *What Do We Know about Jesus?* London: SCM; Philadelphia: Westminster, 1968.

BRAUN, HERBERT. *Jesus: Der Mann aus Nazareth und seine Zeit.* Stuttgart & Berlin: Kreuz-Verlag, 1969.

CARMICHAEL, JOEL. *The Death of Jesus.* New York: Macmillan, 1963. Penguin Books, 1966. Cf. WERNER HARENBERG, *Der Spiegel on the New Testament: A Guide to the Struggle between Radical and Conservative in European University and Parish.* Eng. trans. by James H. Burtness. New York: Macmillan; London: Collier-Macmillan, 1970. On the controversy in Germany when portions of Carmichael's book were published in the magazine, *Der Spiegel;* Conzelmann was among those interviewed. There is also an article by Conzelmann, "Spiegelfechterei um Jesus," in *Christ und Welt* (Stuttgart) 19,8 (25 February, 1966): 10.

CONNICK, C. MILO. *Jesus: The Man, the Mission, and the Message.* Englewood Cliffs, N. J.: Prentice-Hall, 1963.

CRAVERI, MARCELLO. *The Life of Jesus.* Trans. from the Italian by Charles Lam Markman. New York: Grove Press, 1967.

DODD, C. H. *The Founder of Christianity.* New York: Macmillan, 1970; London: Collins, 1971; Fontana Books, 1973.

ENSLIN, MORTON S. *The Prophet from Nazareth.* New York: McGraw-Hill, 1961. Paperback ed., New York: Schocken Books, 1968.

FLUSSER, DAVID. *Jesus in Selbstzeugnissen und Bilddokumenten.* Rowahlts Monographien 140. Reinbeck bei Hamburg, 1968. Eng. trans. by R. Walls. *Jesus.* New York: Herder & Herder, 1969.

HARRISON, EVERETT. *A Short Life of Christ.* Grand Rapids: Eerdmans, 1968.

McCASLAND, S. VERNON. *The Pioneer of Our Faith: A New Life of Jesus.* New York: McGraw-Hill, 1964.

NIEDERWIMMER, KURT. *Jesus.* Göttingen: Vandenhoeck & Ruprecht, 1968.

REUMANN, JOHN. *Jesus in the Church's Gospels: Modern Scholarship and the Earliest Sources.* Philadelphia: Fortress, 1968; London: SPCK, 1970.

SAUNDERS, E. W. *Jesus in the Gospels.* Englewood Cliffs, N. J.: Prentice-Hall, 1967.

SCHONFIELD, HUGH J. *The Passover Plot: New Light on the History of Jesus.* London: Hutchinson; New York: Bernard Geis (Random House), 1966.

SCHWEIZER, EDUARD. *Jesus Christus im vielfältigen Zeugnis des Neuen Testaments.* Munich: Siebenstern Verlag, 1968. Eng. trans. by David E. Green. *Jesus.* London: SCM; Richmond: John Knox, 1971.

SMITH, C. W. F. *The Paradox of Jesus in the Gospels.* Philadelphia: Westminster, 1969.

STAUFFER, ETHELBERT. *Jesus war ganz anders.* Hamburg: Friedrich Witte Verlag, 1967.

Professor CONZELMANN has provided a brief bibliography on "Literature about Jesus" in his *Outline of the Theology of the New Testament* (cited above), pp. 98–99.

2. The Sources:

BEA, AUGUSTIN CARDINAL. *The Study of the Synoptic Gospels: New Approaches and Outlooks.* Eng. trans. ed. J. A. Fitzmyer. New York: Harper & Row; London: Geoffrey Chapman, 1965.

BEARE, F. W. *The Earliest Records of Jesus: A Companion to Huck's 'Synopsis of the First Three Gospels.'* Nashville & New York: Abingdon, 1962. Though often brief and eclectic, this volume, which follows the Synoptic passages in the order in which they are arranged in *Gospel Parallels* (Huck-Lietzmann in the RSV translation), exhibits, more clearly than the often scattered comments in Bultmann's *History of the Synoptic Tradition,* the impact of the historical-critical method on each passage.

CARLSTON, CHARLES E. "A *Positive* Criterion of Authenticity?" *Biblical Research* 7 (1962): 33–44. *NT Abstracts* 13: 757. In contrast to the "negative" criteria of Bultmann, Käsemann, and Conzelmann ("What does *not* parallel current Jewish thought or reflect the interests of the early church may be from Jesus"), this article seeks to authenticate sayings of Jesus by their conformity with his "eschatologically based demand for repentance" and by whether they fit conditions (social, political, ecclesiastical, linguistic) of Jesus' earthly ministry, in contrast to conditions in the post-resurrection church. A tendency to seek "conformity with Jesus' mind and message" and "congruity with his social setting" (cf. the "Chicago School" of American New Testament scholarship, Shailer Mathews, Shirley Jackson Case, et al.) as criteria is to be noted elsewhere too (cf. Keck, cited above under Additional Literature for Section 1).

DUNKERLEY, RODERIC. *Beyond the Gospels.* Penguin Books, 1957. Pp. 24–64. A popular summary, maximalizing noncanonical materials.

FINEGAN, JACK. *Hidden Records of the Life of Jesus.* Philadelphia & Boston: Pilgrim Press, 1969. Rather

104

technical discussion of noncanonical sources, including often full text in Greek, which might shed light on Jesus, with reluctance to pronounce on historicity.

HAENCHEN, ERNST. *Der Weg Jesu: Eine Erklärung des Markus-Evangeliums und der kanonischen Parallelen.* Berlin: Töpelmann, 1966; 2d ed. 1968. An often outstanding treatment of the Synoptic passages in light of Mark.

KEE, HOWARD CLARK. *Jesus in History: An Approach to the Study of the Gospels.* New York: Harcourt, Brace and World, 1970. Pp. 29–61. A more critical discussion of Jesus material within the canon and beyond, designed for college students.

LEHMANN, MARTIN. *Synoptische Quellenanalyse und die Frage nach dem historischen Jesus. Kriterien der Jesusforschung untersucht in Auseinandersetzung mit Emanuel Hirschs "Frühgeschichte des Evangeliums."* BZNW 38 (1970).

McARTHUR, HARVEY K. "Basic Issues: A Survey of Recent Gospel Research." *Interpretation* 18 (1964): 39–55, reprinted in *In Search of the Historical Jesus.* Ed. H. K. McArthur. New York: Scribner's, 1969. Pp. 131–44.

————. "From the Historical Jesus to Christology." *Interpretation* 23 (1969): 190–206. These two articles discuss the question of "criteria" for discerning authentic sayings of Jesus and indicate current views on the matter.

TURNER, H. E. W. *Historicity and the Gospels: A Sketch of the Historical Method and its Application to the Gospels.* London: Mowbray, 1963.

WINTER, PAUL. "Tacitus and Pliny: The Early Christians." *Journal of Historical Studies* 1,1 (Autumn, 1967): 31–40.

————. "Josephus on Jesus." Ibid., 1,4 (Autumn, 1968): 289–302.

3. The World of the Day:

LEIPOLDT, JOHANNES, and WALTER GRUNDMANN. *Umwelt des Urchristentums.* Vol. 1, *Darstellung.* Vol. 2, *Texte.* Vol. 3, *Bilder.* Berlin: Evangelische Verlagsanstalt, 1967.

REICKE, BO. *Neutestamentliche Zeitgeschichte.* Berlin: Töpelmann, 1964. Eng. trans. by David E. Green. *New Testament Era: The World of the Bible from 500 B.C. to A.D. 100.* London: A. & C. Black; Philadelphia: Fortress, 1968. A standard history of the period.

SCHULTZ, HANS JÜRGEN, ed. *Die Zeit Jesu.* Kontexte, Vortragsreihe des Süddeutschen Rundfunks, 3. Stuttgart: Kreuz-Verlag, 1966. Eng. trans. by B. Watchorn. *Jesus in His Time,* with a foreword by William Neil. London: SPCK; Philadelphia: Fortress, 1971. Includes among its chapters, originally given as talks on German radio, Conzelmann's remarks on "The Influence of Jesus after his Death," pp. 142–48.

4. Chronology:

FINEGAN, JACK. *Handbook of Biblical Chronology.* Princeton: Princeton University Press, 1964. Pp. 215–301, on Jesus. Very complete bibliography. The treatment reflects major studies such as those by Holzmeister and Ogg (cited above, in the literature for Section 4) as well as periodical literature.

NINEHAM, D. E., et al. *Historicity and Chronology in the New Testament.* SPCK Theological Collections 6. London: SPCK, 1965. Reprints a number of articles from periodicals, including H. E. W. TURNER, "The Chronological Framework of the Ministry" (pp. 59–74), and GEORGE OGG, "The Chronology of the Last Supper" (pp. 75–96). Generally a more reliable chronology is presumed in the gospels than Conzelmann and other radical critics allow.

RUCKSTUHL, EUGEN. *Die Chronologie des letzten Mahles und des Leidens Jesu.* Einsiedeln & Cologne: Benziger, 1963. Eng. trans. by V. J. Drapela. *Chronology of the Last Days of Jesus: A Critical Study.* New York & Rome: Desclée, 1965. Accepts a longer passion chronology. Cf. Annie Jaubert, *La Date de la Cène: calendrier biblique et liturgique chrétienne* (Paris: Gabalda, 1957); Eng. trans. by I. Rafferty, *The Date of the Last Supper* (Staten Island: Alba House, 1965), whose "two calendar" chronology is rejected by Conzelmann (and the majority of those who have expressed themselves on the issue).

5. Birth and Descent:

BOSLOOPER, THOMAS. *The Virgin Birth*. Philadelphia: Westminster; London: SCM, 1962. A book for the nonspecialist but discusses much recent literature on the topic of Jesus' birth.

JOHNSON, MARSHALL D. *The Purpose of the Biblical Genealogies with Special Reference to the Setting of the Genealogies of Jesus*. SNTSMS 8 (1969). Specialized monograph, with detailed bibliography, on Matthew 1 and Luke 3, considered in the context of "genealogy" as a literary form.

LEANEY, A. R. C. "The Birth Narratives in St Luke and St Matthew." *New Testament Studies* 8 (1961–62): 158–66. *NT Abstracts* 6: 759.

MINEAR, PAUL S. "Luke's Use of the Birth Stories." In *Studies in Luke-Acts: Essays Presented in Honor of Paul Schubert*. Ed. Leander E. Keck and J. Louis Martyn. Nashville & New York: Abingdon, 1966; London: SPCK, 1968. Pp. 111–30.

6. The Locale of the Ministry:

ALT, ALBRECHT, "Die Stätten des Wirkens Jesu in Galiläa territorialgeschichtlich betrachtet." *Beiträge zur biblischen Landes-und Altertumskunde* 68 (1949): 51–72. Reprinted in Alt's *Kleine Schriften zur Geschichte des Volkes Israel* (Munich: Beck), vol. 2 (1955), pp. 436–56. Eng. trans. by Kenneth Grayston. *Where Jesus Worked: Towns and Villages of Galilee Studied with the Help of Local History*. London: Epworth, 1961.

JEREMIAS, JOACHIM. *Jerusalem zur Zeit Jesu*. 3d ed. Göttingen: Vandenhoeck & Ruprecht, 1962. Eng. trans. by F. H. and C. H. Cave. *Jerusalem in the Time of Jesus: An Investigation into Economic and Social Conditions during the New Testament Period*. London: SCM; Philadelphia: Fortress, 1969.

7. Beginnings:

REUMANN, JOHN. "The Quest for the Historical Baptist." In *Understanding the Sacred Text: Essays in Honor of Morton S. Enslin on the Hebrew Bible and Christian Beginnings*. Ed. J. Reumann. Valley Forge, Pa.; Judson Press, 1972. Pp. 181–99. A report on recent research.

SCOBIE, CHARLES H. H. *John the Baptist*. Philadelphia: Fortress, 1964. For the general reader.

WINK, WALTER. *John the Baptist in the Gospel Tradition*. SNTSMS 7 (1968). A more technical examination, along redaction criticism lines.

8. The Circle of Disciples

BETZ, HANS DIETER. *Nachfolge und Nachahmung Jesu Christi im Neuen Testament*. Beiträge zur historischen Theologie 37. Tübingen: Mohr, 1967. "Following Jesus" and "imitating Christ," viewed in light of the theme of *mimesis* in Greek thought and in Paul.

HENGEL, MARTIN. *Nachfolge und Charisma: Eine exegetisch-religionsgeschichtliche Studie zu Mt 8, 21f. und Jesu Ruf in die Nachfolge*. BZNW 34 (1968). More specifically concerned to reach positive conclusions on the historical-Jesus level.

SCHULZ, ANSELM, O. S. B. *Unter dem Anspruch Gottes: Das neutestamentliche Zeugnis von der Nachahmung*. Munich: Kösel Verlag, 1967. A brief summary of a dissertation by a Catholic scholar on "response" to Christ in the New Testament generally.

9. Jesus' Self-Consciousness (Christological Titles):

BALZ, HORST ROBERT. *Methodische Probleme der neutestamentlichen Christologie*. Wissenschaftliche Monographien zum Alten und Neuen Testament 25. Neukirchen-Vluyn: Neukirchener Verlag, 1967.

CONZELMANN, HANS. *Outline of the Theology of the New Testament* (cited above). Pp. 127–37 (Jesus' understanding of himself, a phrase in some ways to be preferred to "self-consciousness"). Pp. 138–40 (the messianic secret).

FULLER, REGINALD H. *The Foundations of New Testament Christology*. New York: Scribner's; London: Lutterworth, 1965. A briefer account, influenced by the work of Hahn (cited below) and others in Germany, but allowing some titles to go back to Jesus, viewed against the Jewish background of the day.

HAHN, FERDINAND. *Christologische Hoheitstitel: Ihre Geschichte im frühen Christentum*. FRLANT 83 (1963). Eng. trans. by Harold Knight and George Ogg. *The Titles of Jesus in Christology: Their History in*

Early Christianity. London: Lutterworth; New York
& Cleveland: World, 1969. Hailed as a definitive study
in Germany, this dissertation deals specifically with
titles in Mark, but at times argues for a historical use
of some (messiological) titles by or about Jesus during
his lifetime.

SABOURIN, LEOPOLD. *The Names and Titles of Jesus:
Themes of Biblical Theology.* Eng. trans. by M.
Carroll. New York: Macmillan, 1967. Analysis by
French Roman Catholic scholar.

TÖDT, HEINZ EDUARD. *Der Menschensohn in der synoptischen Überlieferung.* Gütersloh: Gerd Mohn, 1959;
2d ed. 1963. Eng. trans. by Dorothea M. Barton. *The
Son of Man in the Synoptic Tradition.* London: SCM;
Philadelphia: Westminster, 1965. Major treatment
from the Bultmann school.

VIELHAUER, PHILIPP. "Ein Weg zur neutestamentlichen
Christologie? Prüfung der Thesen Ferdinand Hahns."
Evangelische Theologie 25 (1965): 24–72.

10. The Content of Jesus' Teaching:

CONZELMANN, HANS. "The Idea of God" (in the Synoptics and in the belief of Jesus). In his *Outline of the
Theology of the New Testament* (cited above), pp.
99–106. "The Demand of God." Ibid., pp. 115–27
(bibliography).

HIERS, RICHARD H. *Jesus and Ethics: Four Interpreta-
tions.* Philadelphia: Westminster, 1968. Covers the
views of Harnack, Schweitzer, Bultmann, and Dodd.

JEREMIAS, JOACHIM. *Neutestamentliche Theologie. I.
Teil: Die Verkündigung Jesu.* Gütersloh: Gerd Mohn,
1971. Eng. trans. by John Bowden. *New Testament
Theology. Part One. The Proclamation of Jesus.* London: SCM; New York: Scribner's, 1971.

NEUHÄUSLER, ENGELBERT. *Anspruch und Antwort Gottes:
Zur Lehre von den Weisungen innerhalb der synoptischen Jesusverkündigung.* Düsseldorf: Patmos-Ver-
lag, 1962.

PERRIN, NORMAN. *Rediscovering the Teaching of Jesus*
(cited above, Section 1). Excellent for presenting the
methodology of historical criticism and applying it to
key passages, to recover genuine teachings.

SCHNACKENBURG, RUDOLF. *Die sittliche Botschaft des Neuen Testaments.* 2d rev. ed. Munich: Max Hueber, 1962. Eng. trans. by J. Holland-Smith and W. J. O'Hara. *The Moral Teaching of the New Testament.* Freiburg: Herder; London: Burns & Oates; New York: Herder & Herder, 1965. Pp. 14–167.

Ipsissima Vox Jesu:

SCHÜRMANN, HEINZ. "Die vorösterlichen Anfänge der Logientradition." In *Der historische Jesus und der kerygmatische Christus* (cited below, Section 12), pp. 342–70.

On "Abba," contrast J. JEREMIAS, *The Prayers of Jesus* (SBT 2/6, 1967), pp. 108–12 and 11–65, and *New Testament Theology* (cited above), vol. 1, pp. 36–37 and 61–68, with G. SCHRENK, *"patēr,"* in the *Theological Dictionary of the New Testament* (cited above, under the bibliography of Professor Conzelmann's writings), vol. 5, pp. 945–1067; and CONZELMANN, *Outline of the Theology of the New Testament* (cited above), pp. 101–106, 127–29.

On "Amen," contrast JEREMIAS, *The Prayers of Jesus* (cited above), pp. 112–15, and *New Testament Theology* (cited above), vol. 1, pp. 35–36, with VICTOR HASLER, *Amen: Redaktionsgeschichtliche Untersuchungen zur Einführungsformel des Herrnworte "Wahrlich ich sage euch."* Zurich & Stuttgart: Gotthelf-Verlag, 1969; cf. KLAUS BERGER, *Die Amen-Worte Jesu: Eine Untersuchung zum Problem der Legitimation in apokalyptischer Rede.* BZNW 39 (1970).

The Kingdom:

CONZELMANN, HANS. "The Kingdom of God" (in the Synoptics and in Jesus' usage). In his *Outline of the Theology of the New Testament* (cited above), pp. 106–15 (bibliography).

FLENDER, HELMUT. *Die Botschaft Jesu von der Herrschaft Gottes.* Munich: Chr. Kaiser, 1968.

LADD, GEORGE E. *Jesus and the Kingdom: The Eschatology of Biblical Realism.* New York; Harper & Row, 1964; London: SPCK, 1966. A more conservative treatment but employing the historical approach.

LUNDSTRÖM, GÖSTA. *The Kingdom of God in the Teaching of Jesus: A History of Interpretation from the Last Decades of the Nineteenth Century to the Present Day.* Trans. from the Swedish, *Guds Rike i Jesu Förkunnelse* (Lund: Svenska Kyrkans Diakonistyrelses Bokförlag, 1947), by Joan Bulman, with a postscript by the author. Edinburgh: Oliver & Boyd; Richmond: John Knox, 1963. Provides orientation to recent scholarly views.

PERRIN, NORMAN. *The Kingdom of God in the Teaching of Jesus.* Philadelphia: Westminster; London: SCM, 1963. A standard critical analysis.

SCHNACKENBURG, RUDOLF. *Gottes Herrschaft und Reich.* Freiburg: Herder, 1959. Eng. trans. by John Murray. *God's Rule and Kingdom.* New York: Herder & Herder; Edinburgh & London: Nelson, 1963; London: Search Press, 1968. German Roman Catholic critical summary.

The Parables:

BLACKMAN, E. C. "New Methods of Parable Interpretation." *Canadian Journal of Theology* 15 (1969): 3–13. *NT Abstracts* 14: 462.

EICHHOLZ, GEORG. *Einführung in die Gleichnisse.* Biblische Studien 37. Neukirchen-Vluyn: Neukirchener Verlag, 1963. A not overly technical introduction.

LINNEMANN, ETA. *Gleichnisse Jesu: Einführung und Auslegung.* Göttingen: Vandenhoeck & Ruprecht, 1961; 3d ed. 1964. Eng. trans. *Parables of Jesus: Introduction and Exposition.* London: SPCK, 1966. American edition, *Jesus of the Parables: Introduction and Exposition.* New York: Harper & Row, 1967. Treats selected parables, for teaching purposes, along existential lines of interpretation.

ROBINSON, JAMES M. "Jesus' Parables as God Happening." In *Jesus and the Historian: Written in Honor of Ernest Cadman Colwell.* Ed. F. Thomas Trotter. Philadelphia: Westminster, 1968. Pp. 134–50.

VIA, DAN OTTO, JR. *The Parables: Their Literary and Existential Dimension.* Philadelphia: Fortress, 1967.

111

CONZELMANN, HANS. *Outline of the Theology of the New Testament* (cited above), pp. 120–23 (on the "antitheses").

DAVIES, W. D. *The Setting of the Sermon on the Mount.* New York: Cambridge University Press, 1964. A detailed series of studies, with extensive bibliography. A popularized version, omitting many of the notes, appears in the same author's *The Sermon on the Mount* (Cambridge University Press, 1966).

NEUHÄUSLER, E. *Anspruch und Antwort Gottes* (cited above, in the general literature for this section).

WREGE, H.-T. *Die Überlieferungsgeschichte der Bergpredigt.* Wissenschaftliche Untersuchungen zum Neuen Testament 9. Tübingen: Mohr, 1968.

The Miracles:

BULTMANN, RUDOLF. "The Question of Wonder" (1933 in the original German). Eng. trans. by Louise Pettibone Smith, in *Faith and Understanding I,* ed. R. Funk. New York: Harper & Row, 1969. Pp. 247–61.

CONZELMANN, HANS. *Outline of the Theology of the New Testament* (cited above), pp. 137–38 (bibliography).

FRIDRICHSEN, ANTON. *Le problème du miracle dans le Christianisme primitif.* Strasbourg, 1925. Eng. trans. by Roy Harrisville and John S. Hanson. *The Problem of Miracle in Primitive Christianity.* With a foreword by Krister Stendahl. Minneapolis: Augsburg, 1972.

FULLER, REGINALD H. *Interpreting the Miracles.* Philadelphia: Westminster, 1963. Brief, more recent treatment, reflecting form and redaction criticism.

KELLER, ERNST and MARIE-LUISE. *Der Streit um die Wunder.* Gütersloh: Gerd Mohn, 1968. Eng. trans. by Margaret Kohl. *Miracles in Dispute: A Continuing Debate.* London: SCM; Philadelphia: Fortress, 1969. Bibliography. Helpful on how miracles have been interpreted, especially in modern scholarship.

LOOS, H. VAN DER. *The Miracles of Jesus.* Supplements to Novum Testamentum 9. Leiden: Brill, 1965. Fairly detailed, sometimes apologetically concerned.

RICHARDSON, ALAN. *The Miracle Stories of the Gospels.* New York: Harper, 1941; London: SCM, many editions. A standard and able examination of how theologically inclined, historical scholarship treats the miracles of Jesus.

11. The Passion:

BAMMEL, ERNST, ed. *The Trial of Jesus: Cambridge Studies in honour of C. F. D. Moule.* SBT 2/13, 1970. A series of essays by Bammel, Catchpole, and other friends and pupils of Professor Moule, of Cambridge, generally seeking to establish greater historicity for the Sanhedrin trial than is usually conceded by critical scholars.

BRANDON, S. G. F. *The Trial of Jesus of Nazareth.* Historic Trials Series. London: Batsford; New York: Stein & Day, 1968. Popular, booklength presentation of a position presented in numerous articles by Brandon, that Jesus was a political revolutionist put to death by the Romans.

CATCHPOLE, DAVID R. *The Trial of Jesus: A Study in the Gospels and in Jewish Historiography from 1770 to the Present Day.* Studia Post-Biblica 18. Leiden: Brill, 1971.

GORDIS, ROBERT, ed. "The Trial of Jesus in the Light of History: A Symposium." *Judaism* 20,1 (winter, 1971): 6–74. Essays by HAIM COHN, MORTON S. ENSLIN, DAVID FLUSSER, ROBERT M. GRANT, S. G. F. BRANDON, J. BLINZLER, G. SLOYAN, and SAMUEL SANDMEL (most of whom have written extensively on the subject elsewhere).

HENGEL, MARTIN. *War Jesus Revolutionär?* Calwer Hefte 110. Stuttgart: Calwer Verlag, 1970. Eng. trans. by W. Klassen. *Was Jesus a Revolutionist?* FBBS 28 (1971). Bibliography.

LINNEMANN, ETA. *Studien zur Passionsgeschichte.* Göttingen: Vandenhoeck & Ruprecht, 1970. Claims that the passion story circulated during the oral period in brief units, not in one sustained account as form critics have held.

LOHSE, EDUARD. *Die Geschichte des Leidens und Sterbens Jesu Christi.* Gütersloh: Gerd Mohn, 1964. Eng. trans. by Martin O. Dietrich. *History of the Suffering and Death of Jesus Christ.* Philadelphia: Fortress, 1967. A somewhat popular summary of the view generally held in German scholarship by a then colleague of

Conzelmann at Göttingen who is now bishop of the Church of Hannover.

SHERWIN-WHITE, A. N. *Roman Society and Roman Law in the New Testament.* New York: Oxford University Press, 1963. Pp. 24–47, "The Trial of Christ in the Synoptic Gospels," defend traditional views as basically historical in light of Roman practices involved.

TAYLOR, VINCENT. *The Passion Narrative of St Luke: A Critical and Historical Investigation.* Ed. O. E. Evans. SNTSMS 19 (1972). On the basis of the proto-Luke theory and special sources, the reliability of the Lukan version is claimed.

VIERING, F., ed. *Zur Bedeutung des Todes Jesu.* Gütersloh: Gerd Mohn, 1967 (cited fully in the writings of Hans Conzelmann, above). Eng. trans. in *Interpretation* 24,2 (April, 1970): "Understanding the Death of Jesus: *The Report of the Theological Committee of the* Evangelischen Kirchen der Union," pp. 139–50; E. Käsemann, "The Pauline Theology of the Cross," pp. 151–77; H. Conzelmann, "History and Theology in the Passion Narratives of the Synoptic Gospels," pp. 178–97; E. Haenchen, "History and Interpretation in the Johannine Passion Narrative," pp. 198–219; Walter Kreck, "The Word of the Cross: Doctrinal Theses and Definitions Dealing with the Death of Jesus in Current Theology and Proclamation," pp. 220–42. Papers from a study initiated by the Evangelische Kirche der Union in Germany, a study which also produced the essays in W. Marxsen et al., *The Significance of the Message of the Resurrection* (cited below, Section 12).

WILSON, WILLIAM RILEY. *The Execution of Jesus: A Judicial, Literary and Historical Investigation.* New York: Scribner's, 1970.

WINTER, PAUL. *On the Trial of Jesus.* Studia Judaica 1. Berlin: de Gruyter, 1961. A series of important historical studies by a scholar of Jewish background who follows the form-critical method.

12. The Historical Jesus and Faith (Jesus of Nazareth and Jesus Christ) :

ACHTEMEIER, PAUL J. *An Introduction to the New Hermeneutic.* Philadelphia: Westminster, 1969. Provides a survey of the movement which grew out of the "new quest," especially as Fuchs and others interpreted Jesus and his word.

BULTMANN, RUDOLF. "The Primitive Christian Kerygma and the Historical Jesus," lecture to the Heidelberg Academy, June 25, 1959. Eng. trans. in C. E. Braaten and R. A. Harrisville, eds., *The Historical Jesus and the Kerygmatic Christ: Essays on the New Quest of the Historical Jesus*. Nashville & New York: Abingdon, 1964. Pp. 15–42. Bultmann's famed response to the "new quest": while a bit more might be said regarding Jesus than Bultmann's 1926 "life" did, it is wrong to seek more than the "dass" of Jesus' existence—i.e., the fact that there was a man named Jesus of Nazareth who was put to death by the Romans, etc., but whose own view of his death we do not know; it is wrong theologically and in terms of the use of the sources.

FULLER, REGINALD H. *The Formation of the Resurrection Narratives.* New York: Macmillan, 1971; London: SPCK, 1972.

HAHN, FERDINAND, WENZEL LOHFF, and GÜNTHER BORNKAMM. *Die Frage nach dem historischen Jesus.* Ed. Paul Rieger. Evangelisches Forum 2. Göttingen: Vandenhoeck & Ruprecht, 1962. Eng. trans. by Grover Farley. *What Can We Know about Jesus? Essays on the New Quest.* Philadelphia: Fortress, 1969.

JÜNGEL, EBERHARD. *Paulus und Jesus: Eine Untersuchung zur Präzisierung der Frage nach dem Ursprung der Christologie.* Hermeneutische Untersuchungen zur Theologie 2. Tübingen: Mohr; 1962, 2d ed. 1964. Summarized in the review article by James M. Robinson in *Interpretation* 18 (1964): 347–59. Jüngel finds that, though the self-consciousness of the historical Jesus is not the same as the outlook of the early church's Christology, there are connections between Jesus and what we find in Paul.

KÄSEMANN, ERNST. "Sackgassen im Streit um den historischen Jesus." *Exegetische Versuche und Besinnungen,* vol. 2. Göttingen: Vandenhoeck & Ruprecht, 1964. Pp. 31–68. Eng. trans. by W. J. Montague, "Blind Alleys in the 'Jesus of History' Controversy," in Käsemann's volume of essays, *New Testament Ques-*

tions of Today. London: SCM; Philadelphia: Fortress, 1969. Pp. 23–65. Käsemann's rejection of the approaches of Jeremias, Stauffer, and others in historical-Jesus studies. He himself has thus repudiated much that passes for the quest he initiated.

MARXSEN, WILLI. *Anfangsprobleme der Christologie.* Gütersloh: Gerd Mohn, 1960. Eng. trans. by Paul J. Achtemeier. *The Beginnings of Christology: A Study in Its Problems.* FBBS 22 (1969). Bibliography. Attempts to find links for the church's Christology back to the historical Jesus.

————. *Die Auferstehung Jesu von Nazareth.* Gütersloh: Gerd Mohn, 1968. Eng. trans. by Margaret Kohl. *The Resurrection of Jesus of Nazareth.* London: SCM; Philadelphia: Fortress, 1970.

MARXSEN, WILLI, ULRICH WILCKENS, GERHARD DELLING, and HANS-GEORG GEYER. *Die Bedeutung der Auferstehungsbotschaft für den Glauben an Jesus Christus.* Ed. Fritz Viering. Gütersloh: Gerd Mohn, 1966. Eng. trans. by Dorothea M. Barton and R. A. Wilson. *The Significance of the Message of the Resurrection for Faith in Jesus Christ.* Ed. C. F. D. Moule. SBT 2/8 (1968). Cf. the notation above, in Section 11, on F. Viering, ed., *Zur Bedeutung des Todes Jesu,* which is a parallel study on the significance of the message of the death of Jesus for faith in Jesus Christ.

RISTOW, H., and K. MATTHIAE, eds. *Der historische Jesus und der kerygmatische Christus.* Berlin: Evangelische Verlagsanstalt, 1961. Some 48 essays by various scholars on the quest.

ROBINSON, JAMES M. *Kerygma und historischer Jesus.* Zurich & Stuttgart: Zwingli Verlag, 1960. Expanded German trans. of Robinson's *A New Quest of the Historical Jesus* (cited above, Section 12).

————. "The Recent Debate on the 'New Quest.'" *Journal of Bible and Religion* 30 (1962): 198–208.

SCHUBERT, KURT, ed. *Der historische Jesus und der Christus unseres Glaubens: Eine katholische Auseinandersetzung mit den Folgen der Entmythologisierungstheorie.* Vienna & Freiburg: Herder, 1962. A collection of essays by Roman Catholics on the "new quest."